PATRICK & BEATRICE HAGGERTY LIBRARY
MOUNT MARY COLLEGE
MILWAUKEE, WISCONSIN 53222

WITHDRAWN

S0-BSE-439

SAINT STANISŁAW, Bishop of Kraków

PATRICK & BEATRICE HAGGERTY LIBRARY
MOUNT MARY COLLEGE
MILWAUKEE, WISCONSIN 53222

SAINT STANISŁAW

Bishop of Kraków

IN COMMEMORATION

of the 900th Anniversary of His Martyrdom

in 1079

With a Foreword by

John Cardinal Krol, Archbishop

of Philadelphia

Saint Stanisław Publications Committee

Under the Auspices of the Polish American Historical Association
California Chapter
Santa Barbara ✦ 1979 ✦ California

Printed in the United States of America
Library of Congress Catalog Number 79-65592
ISBN 0-9602944-0-6

921
St246
c.2

DEDICATED TO HIS HOLINESS

POPE JOHN PAUL II

CONTENTS

JOHANNES PAULUS, P.P. II

◄ Left: The Pope's Coat of Arms

FOREWORD

THE CALIFORNIA Chapter of the Polish American Historical Association in this book pays tribute to two former bishops of Kraków. It commemorates the 900th anniversary of the death of Bishop Stanisław, and the election of the Cardinal Archbishop Karol Wojtyła of Kraków to the Papacy.

Canonized saints have in a sense made the Church's Hall of Fame. The saints are presented as models for our inspiration and imitation, and as powerful intercessors before the throne of God. They are not simply reminders of a distant past, but are living members of the Church united with us in the Communion of Saints.

The life of Saint Stanisław is better known from a rich oral tradition than from primary source documentation. The tradition was recorded by such chroniclers as Gall and Bishop Wincenty Kadłubek who wrote around 1115 and 1208 respectively. Sparse primary sources serve as an invitation to some historians to speculate about unrecorded details, to theorize, and at times to build "castles on ice." According to reliable sources Stanisław of Szczepanówa was born in 1030; became the Bishop of Kraków in 1072 and was martyred by order of King Bolesław II the Daring on 11 April 1079. The popular reaction against this crime caused the king to go into exile. Poland was placed under interdict. In 1089 the body of Stanisław was transferred to the cathedral. His cult spread rapidly in and beyond Poland as is evident from a twelfth century image in the baptistry of Tryde in Sweden. He was formally canonized on 8 September 1253 by Pope Innocent IV in the Basilica of Saint Francis of Assisi.

Stanisław was a highly intelligent and zealous apostle, an indefatigable preacher and courageous in promoting Christian morals and discipline.

Bolesław the Daring evinced many fine qualities of character and leadership, but in time these were eclipsed by unbridled lust and savage cruelty. There is evidence of a strain of psychic illness in his maternal ancestors. Bishop Stanisław reproached Bolesław for abuse of power and violation of human rights and placed him under formal sentence of excommunication. The king became enraged and ordered Stanisław slain. The king and his guards killed and dismembered the body of the bishop in the chapel of Saint Mickał.

In his *Sketches of the Eleventh Century*, written in 1904, Professor Tadeusz Wojciechowski, focusing attention only on a word used in the chronicle of Gall, raises the question of whether the bishop had been involved in an insurrection against the king and was killed for treason.

In this connection it will help to recall that Thomas More, Thomas Becket, and John Fisher, were all charged with treason and executed by a king. In the case of Stanisław, such a charge may have been leveled, but it was a popular conviction that he was a martyr and not a victim of just punishment. The transfer of Stanisław's remains to the cathedral ten years after his death, his cult which spread in and beyond Poland, the interdict placed on Poland and his eventual canonization, are facts which do not bear out the charge of treason.

The election of the former Cardinal Archbishop of Kraków to the Papal throne amazed and delighted the world. It was the first time in history that a Pole was so elected. His election broke a tradition of over 450 years of Italian popes. And yet, in 1848, the poet Juliusz Słowacki wrote the poem "Pósród Niesnasek Pan Bóg Uderza" in which he described the election and the activity of a Slav pope—a brother of the people—who will cast God's love on all peoples.

It is my fervent hope that this book will pay due tribute to the two Bishops of Kraków, and will help its readers to have a better understanding and appreciation of the history of Poland and of its people.

✝ John Cardinal Krol
ARCHBISHOP OF PHILADELPHIA

March 4, 1979
Feast of Saint Casimir

SAINT STANISŁAW
Bishop and Martyr: Fact and Legend

THE LIFE of Saint Stanisław, bishop and martyr, patron saint of Poland, is shrouded in mystery. Sources of information on the eleventh century prelate are so meager that this circumstance has occasioned a lively and interesting polemic among Polish scholars which continues to this day. Conscious of their imprisonment to the few sources available, they have unhesitatingly labelled their often masterly expositions as "hypotheses."

None of the sources available on any aspect of the life of Saint Stanisław is a contemporary source. The chronicle of Gallus Anonymus, the work of an unknown French monk who wandered into Poland around 1086, and established himself in the court of Duke Bolesław Krzywousty (the Wrymouth) at the turn of the century, is the basic source of information on the most important episode in the bishop's life, his death, and its consequences.

Even the national origin of this enigmatic author is not without its mystery. However, it can be stated with some confidence that his valuable chronicle must have been written sometime between 1113 and 1117, or about a generation after the death of the saint. His information, though not contemporary, must have been garnered from men who were younger contemporaries of Saint Stainsław.

Another source on the death of the saint is the thirteenth century chronicler, Master Wincenty Kadłubek, Bishop of Kraków from 1208 to 1218. The differences between the two chronicles reflect the changed conditions between the early twelfth century and the early thirteenth century. Above all, Gallus Anonymus wrote in the midst of the con-

15

tinuing struggle over investitures. The Church in Poland, in common with the churches of western Europe, had not felt the effect of the Gregorian reform program. Master Wincenty, on the other hand, was consecrated bishop by the reform-minded Gregorian disciplinary enthusiast, Archbishop Henryk Kietlicz. The triumphal ascendancy of the Church in Europe is clearly visible in Master Wincenty's chronicle. Whereas the earlier chronicle is a panegyric to his master, Duke Bolesław the Wrymouth, Master Wincenty's chronicle is didactic, and in part hagiographic, motivated by the desire to build a cult around the memory of one of his predecessors as Bishop of Kraków, Saint Stanisław.

Aside from the obvious differences between the two chronicles, they are joined by Master Wincenty's extensive reliance on Gallus Anonymus. Kadłubek's chronicle not only uses the information in the Anonymus's chronicle, but embellishes and expands on it. In the strict sense, therefore, Master Wincenty's chronicle cannot be considered a primary source on the events of the saint's life. He does follow a tradition handed down from the days of the early Piast rulers concerning the customs of the Polish clans, but his exposition of the life of Saint Stanisław is a mixture of fact and legend which was usual for chroniclers of his time. In spite of these reservations, the chronicle of Master Wincenty Kadłubek cannot be dismissed, inasmuch as he was a native Pole, unlike the Anonymus, and therefore had a better "feel" for the traditions of his native land than his earlier literary compatriot.

Beyond Gallus Anonymus and Kadłubek, the "sources" are two *Lives* of Saint Stanisław, a shorter version and a lengthier version, both of them attributed to a Dominican friar, Wincenty of Kiecle. Hagiographical in intent and style, the two *Lives*, in spite of wide disagreement as to the dates of their appearance, seem to have been part of the canonization campaign which was waged in the reign of Pope Innocent IV (1243–1254). The canonization process itself, undertaken through the active support of Bishop Prandota of Kraków, resulted in the formation of a canonization commission under the Franciscan James of Velletri. The resulting *Miracula* of Saint Stanisław, as well as the canonization bull of Pope Innocent IV, dated at Assisi, 17 September 1253, form the final group of "sources" on the life of Stanisław of Szczepanów. Their debt to the Anonymus and to Master Wincenty are obvious, repeating for posterity the main lines of a picture of the bishop which lasted, without much challenge, until the rise of rational historical inquiry in the late nineteenth century in Poland.

The above-mentioned chronicles, *Lives* and *Miracula*, concentrate their attention on the tragic circumstances of the saint's death, so that we are left with scattered pieces of information of an indirect nature on his family background, his character, and his assumption of the episcopal see of Kraków. Aside from his birthplace in the village of Szczepanów, near the town of Bochnia, east of Kraków, little is known of his family background, childhood, or education. One group of Polish historians, led by Tadeusz Wojciechowski and Stanisław Ketrzyński, defend the thesis that he sprang from the noble family of Turzyn which had land holdings in the Bochnia area. Another thesis, most recently articulated by Witold Sawicki, places his ancestry as a nephew of King Bolesław the Bold through his mother and as a grandson of the brother of the Polish king's mother, Dobronega, who was, in turn, the daughter of Duke Vladimir the Great of Kiev. The strongest argument in favor of the latter claim that Saint Stanisław was of royal lineage was the tendency for the ruler to surround himself with relatives in the most important offices of his court and the Church.

The date of Saint Stanisław's birth has not definitely been established, but wide agreement exists that he was born in the early 1040's. This would mean that he was a young man in his early thirties when he assumed the episcopal seat at Kraków. The thirteenth century *Lives* of the saint characterize him as learned, just and severe, a zealous pastor. The *Lives* also commit the chronological error of placing him as a student at a French university, though the first universities did not arise until the end of the twelfth century. Perhaps this traditional tale of university study in France need not be discarded as it is entirely possible that the thirteenth century chronicler, Wincenty of Kielce had, in fact, used contemporary terminology to describe the monastic schools of the eleventh century.

The moment of Saint Stanisław's appointment by Duke Bolesław the Bold as Bishop of Kraków in 1072 was a critical one. The Church in Poland was a young one, organizationally less than a century old. Moreover, a sharp pagan reaction had convulsed the "first state" of the Piast dynasty in the third decade of the eleventh century and had shaken the foundation of both the monarchy and the Church. Opinion is sharply divided on the extent of the damage done to ecclesiastical institutions by this pagan reaction. No one, however, doubts that the extent of that crisis in the Church was such that it required extensive rebuilding. The crisis of the monarchy and the Church was further complicated by the Czech Duke Brétislav II who, taking advantage of the weakness of the Piast lands, took Silesia, invaded the metropolitan see of Gniezno and carried off the reliquary remains of Saint Wojciech (Adalbert), missionary bishop to the Pomeranians and authentic Christian martyr.

The effects of the pagan reaction and the Czech invasion had much greater consequences in the bishoprics of northern Poland, that is, the Archdiocese of Gniezno and the dioceses of Poznań and Kołobrzeg. Indeed, some authorities claim that the metropolitan see of Gniezno had ceased to function. The diocese of Kraków was much less affected by the pagan reaction than the northern dioceses, and it was to this city that Kazimierz Odnowiciel (the Restorer) returned from his German exile. Restoration of both ducal and ecclesiastical authority was an enormous task in spite of the continuity with the past that the Kraków diocese was able to provide. Nor was it possible for Kazimierz the Restorer to achieve that restoration alone, relying on Polish resources.

The clergy of Poland was decimated and the damage wrought to the sees of Gniezno and Poznań forced the young and energetic duke to seek aid from far-off Rome, in order to seek a consecrating bishop. The ties that bound Poland and Rome of necessity had to be rebuilt.

Kazimierz the Restorer had not completed the task of restoration before his death in 1058. Much of the credit must be given to his successor, Duke Bolesław the Bold. The moment was propitious: signs of a revived Papacy and the antecedents of the Gregorian reform program were already visible in western Europe by the middle of the eleventh century. It would be impossible here to discuss the wide ramifications of the conflict over investitures, even as that celebrated conflict touched on Polish affairs. However, it will be sufficient to emphasize that a primary goal of the monk Hildebrand, later Pope Gregory VII, leading the reformers, was upgrading the quality of the episcopal and clerical order.

Why did Duke Bolesław the Bold appoint Stanisław of Szczepanów as Bishop of Kraków in 1072? None of the sources previously cited shed any light on this subject. Several plausible inferences are possible. The pre-Gregorian Church was accustomed to the habit of lay appointment and investiture of bishops; therefore we must seek our explanations in the plans of Duke Bolesław himself. There is no doubt that his highest priority was regaining the royal crown of the Piasts, first given to his great grandfather, Bolesław the Brave, in 1025. A pro-papal policy emerged, not only because it became the only possible vehicle for the coronation of Bolesław the Bold, but also because it was entirely consistent with the policy and the tradition established in the tenth century by Dukes Mieszko I and Bolesław I the Brave. If Witold Sawicki's thesis, that Stanisław of Szczepanów was, indeed, a nephew of Bolesław the Bold, can be accepted, this would merely add to the hypothesis here presented that Stanisław was himself one of the cogs in the campaign to regain the royal crown through papal intervention. The desire of Bolesław the Bold to acquire a royal crown merges with Gregory VII's desire to upgrade the life of the clergy. Stanisław of Szczepanów was, therefore, no ordinary, pre-Gregorian choice for the most important Polish bishopric of that time. There is, of course, no evidence that Bolesław had ever applied to Rome for permission to install Stanisław in the see of Kraków, nor was such a procedure usual in the pre-Gregorian Church. Bolesław the Bold's own activity on behalf of the Church in Poland— the rebuilding of Poznań cathedral, the founding of the Benedictine monastery of Mogilno, and ultimately the reconstruction of the Church's organization—indicated a mind in tune with the mind of Gregory VII. Could he have chosen a man to an important bishopric any less committed to Gregorian ideals? The foregoing hypothesis buttresses the picture given to us in the *Lives* of a "learned, just and severe, and zealous pastor."

The letter of Pope Gregory VII to Duke Bolesław the Bold, dated 20 April 1075, sheds some light on Bolesław's relations with the bishop. The letter itself may conveniently be divided into three parts: the first part complains about the lack of a metropolitan see for Poland and the inadequate number of bishoprics for so vast a territory. The second part mentions that, besides those matters already broached, there are others about which he will not write, but which need immediate attention, for which purpose he is sending his legates to Poland. The third part of the letter refers to the treasure chest of the Ruthenian Duke Iziaslav which Bolesław the Bold purportedly stole from him and which Gregory VII admonishes him to return.

What were those "other matters" about which the pope did not wish to discuss? They must have been more important matters than the two questions which he does discuss in the first and third parts. Hypothetically, the questions were probably not related to the Polish duke's relations with Gregory's adversary, Emperor Henry IV, for there was no danger whatsoever of Bolesław's defection to the imperial camp in the developing struggle over investitures. These "other matters" could not include the division of the vast Kraków diocese in order to establish the diocese of Płock for the missionary territory of Mazovia. Such a matter would obviously be included in the subject matter of the first part of the letter. By a process of elimination, the subject was probably an internal matter, and probably the beginnings of a serious rift between Duke Bolesław the Bold and Bishop Stanisław.

Mme. Karolina Lanckorońska has advanced the hypothesis that the dispute between the two authorities centered around the desire of Bolesław to advance his political designs eastward toward Ruthenia by renewing a purported, but lost diocese of the Slavic rite in Mazovia which would sharply reduce the vast territory of the Kraków diocese, hence the deterioration of relations between the duke and the bishop. Here also, the desire to create another diocese or renew an old one is covered in the first item in the pope's letter. There is, indeed, a relationship between Bolesław's desire for a royal crown and his ability to wield greater influence eastward which might explain his desire to separate Mazovia from the Kraków diocese, thus precipitating a confrontation with Bishop Stanisław. However, it should be pointed out that Bolesław received the royal crown and was duly crowned and anointed king of Poland on Christmas Day, 1076, one month before Emperor Henry IV went to Canossa to offer his submission to Pope Gregory VII. Thus, it would seem that papal-imperial relations had more bearing on the coronation than Bolesław's forays eastward.

The text of the letter also indicates the pope's desire to re-establish the metropolitan authority of Gniezno and the organization of the Polish episcopate around Gniezno. This was not "another matter" not covered in Gregory's first item so that Gregory's agenda merely tantalizes us, but does not solve the problem of the deterioration of relations between king and bishop.

Whatever the issues in this deterioration of relations were, the fact is that the bishop of the diocese of Kraków, Stanisław of Szczepanów, was on 11 April 1079 cruelly and barbarously murdered and quartered in the church of Saint Stephen outside Kraków by royal henchmen, and quite possibly with the participation of the king, Bolesław the Bold himself. The cryptic comment of the one source closest to the event, the chronicle of Gallus Anonymus, has occasioned a centuries-long debate in popular and scholarly literature concerning the causes of this brutal act. The quotation from the chronicle is here rendered in translation thus:

> As for the events leading to the exile of King Bolesław from Poland, we could say much. This at least we can say, that being himself anointed of the Lord, he should not have punished corporally another one anointed of the Lord for any sin whatever. This act harmed him very much since one sin followed another sin, and for treason he ordered the bishop quartered. We, however, neither justify the bishop-traitor nor do we defend the king who used his rights so hideously—but let us leave these matters and consider how he was received in Hungary.

The chronicle of Master Wincenty Kadłubek, more than a century later, provides us with an embellishment of the Anonymus's remarks that King Bolesław had cruelly maltreated his knights and their wives and for this, the "learned, just, severe and zealous pastor," Bishop Stanisław, excommunicated him. Thereupon, in a rage the king killed the bishop. Master Wincenty's interpretation found its way into the hagiographic literature of the thirteenth century whereas the fifteenth century Polish chronicler Jan Długosz made Kadłubek's version even more specific by claiming that the king committed adultery with Krystyna, the wife of one of his knights Mścisław, supposedly of the House of Rurik. Długosz further claims that the bishop also came forth in defense of other adulteress-wives of knights who were cruelly used by the king as well as in defense of knights who deserted the king while on military expeditions in foreign lands.

The Kadłubek version of the events leading to King Bolesław's downfall remained the traditional, centuries-long belief of Poles until the rise of critical historical research in the late nineteenth century. The firm ties that were to bind the Roman Church in Poland to the people developed an ecclesiastical consciousness which would regard as suspect any other interpretation.

In 1904 Professor Tadeusz Wojciechowski published his now famous *Sketches of the Eleventh Century* in which he again introduced the question of the death of Saint Stanisław in several articles. Applying the rigorous critical standards of positivist historiography, Wojciechowski insisted that the key to unravelling the mystery of the bishop's death still lay in an interpretation of the chronicle closest to the event. He regarded the much later chronicle of Master Wincenty as a product of a cultist mentality on its way to marshaling evidence for the bishop's canonization. After much reflection, Wojciechowski came to the conclusion that the bishop was guilty of treason and that his treason was associated with his relations to the imperial-Czech camp in a plot to remove King Bolesław in favor of his brother, Wladysław Herman, on the throne. The key word in Gallus's account of the event is *traditio-traditor*. The classical Latin dictionary of Du Cange used by Wojciechowski defined the term as treason, which means plotting with external enemies to the detriment of one's own country. It is a rigid, literal interpretation which admits of no other possible interpretation in the medieval Latin then in use.

The impressive display of historical method and erudition quickly found for Wojciechowski a host of defenders, but also many opponents. The two camps measured each other and in 1909, the implacable foe of the Wojciechowski hypothesis, Professor Kazimierz Krotoski, arranged for an "inquest" into the problem of the murder of Saint Stanisław which was conducted in the pages of the journal *Przegląd Powszechny* [the Universal Review]. This concentrated attack on the Wojciechowski hypothesis involved some of Poland's leading historians: Wojciech Kętrzyński, Antoni Prochaska, and especially the great Stanisław Smolka. Individually, this collection of historians and philologists attacked the Wojciechowski hypothesis on two grounds: that the king's brother, Wladysław Herman, took no part in the revolt against him, since there was no revolt, merely a revulsion of a whole people against his murder of the bishop; second, that Saint Stanisław fell victim to a martyr's death in circumstances which cannot be unravelled because of the cryptic nature of the Anonymus's testimony. Nor, as Professor Smolka claimed, would we ever likely be in a position to know without the aid of new evidence.

Professor Wojciechowski defended himself of these charges with sarcastic erudition, thus stoking the fires of further debate. He was accused by his adversaries of making wilful and unwarranted changes in the text of Gallus Anonymus in a crucial passage: where the text clearly stated that "this at least must be said that a Christian ought not to punish Christians corporally for any sins whatever," Wojciechowski had emended the text to read that "this at least must be said that an anointed ought not to punish an anointed corporally for any sins whatever." The distinction was in the Latin phrases *christianus in christianos* and *christianus in christianum.* The charge against Wojciechowski was twofold: that his historical methodology was inadmissible in changing the Latin terminology, and that *christianus in christianum* does not translate into "annointed." Thus, practically, the difference in interpretation between the two camps is fundamental: the anti-Wojciechowski camp defended the position that the king had been driven from the throne for his cruelty to "Christians," i.e., the whole people; Wojciechowski, on the other hand, isolated the issue as one between two anointed persons, king and bishop.

Wojciechowski's reply to these charges was published in Poland's leading historical journal, *Kwartalnik Historyczny* [Historical Quarterly] the following year. He sought to understand the translation given by his adversaries, but it made no sense to him since Christians did, in fact, corporally punish other Christians for sins. More to the point, he claimed that a serious error in textual copy was made by a fifteenth century copyist whereas a fourteenth century copyist had correctly deciphered the original.

Professor Wojciechowski received support for his position from Professor Stanisław Krzyżanowski in the same edition of the *Historical Journal*, following his own defense. Krzyżanowski brought his vast knowledge of textual criticism into play by criticizing both sides for using a copy of Gallus prepared by the German scholar Bandtkie, whereas, in fact, a copy, more faithful to the original, discovered in 1847 and known as *Codex Zamojski* existed but was ignored by both camps. This ignoring he attributed to the pervasive influence on Polish historiography of the *Monumenta Poloniae Historica*, which is Poland's major collection of historical sources on the medieval period. The *Monumenta* simply repeated the error of copying *christianus in christianos* whereas the *Codex Zamojski* copy had *christianus in christianum*. Thus, without the benefit of an accurate copy of Gallus, Krzyżanowski commended Wojciechowski for his historical sense in recognizing the error.

Professor Wojciechowski then charged that his adversaries had also committed wilful methodological liberties by relying on the chronicle of Master Wincenty Kadłubek, more than a century later than Gallus. They were forced into this untenable position by the realization that the chronicle of Gallus Anonymus could not support their position that Bishop Stanisław was murdered by the king for opposing his tyranny. There were, of course, further considerations relating to the aftermath of the murder. King Bolesław the Bold was driven into exile in Hungary and again, the Anonymus chronicle is not clear on several points: Was the king driven from his throne immediately by an uprising? How did his cousin, Ladislaus, king of Hungary, receive him? What was the role of the king's brother, Wladysław Herman, in the supposed plot against him? These are important questions for a fuller understanding of the conflict between king and bishop, though peripheral to the parameters of this essay.

Both camps were at least united on one point: new evidence was needed to unravel the mystery of the confrontation. Thus, in 1926 Professor Wladysław Semkowicz published an article in which he claimed that new evidence of an iconographic character had been discovered to reopen the debate on the "problem of Saint Stanisław." The Swedish art historian, Jan Roosval had, in several publications, claimed to have uncovered a baptismal font in the Swedish village of Tryde, in the southern Swedish province of Scania, which, in the bas-reliefs surrounding the font, depicted the "legend of Saint Stanisław." Professor Semkowicz accepted Roosval's claim that the bas-reliefs on the baptismal font originated in the twelfth century, earlier than Master Wincenty's chronicle, therefore, more trustworthy than Kadłubek, for the Wojciechowski camp had charged that the role of the early thirteenth century chronicler was to begin consciously a cult in honor of the bishop, eventually leading to his canonization. Indeed, it was claimed that if a cult of veneration had begun, it arose quietly, naturally and earlier than the thirteenth century, thus disposing of the charge that Master Wincenty's role was artificially to initiate the cult.

The bas-reliefs surrounding the baptismal font supposedly depicted several legends in the life of the saint which parallel those depicted in the *Lives* of the thirteenth century. Both bas-relief and the *Lives* show Saint Stanisław being sentenced by a court to be quartered, though there is no other evidence to prove that any legal process, canonical or civil, was ever held. More interesting was the depiction in both sources of the legend of the resurrection of a certain Peter from whom the bishop was supposed to have purchased some land in the village of Piotrawin. Soon after, Peter died and his nephews claimed the land anew since the bishop had not paid for the land. The case was appealed to King Bolesław for judgment, and since no witnesses for the defense were permitted, Saint Stanisław caused the dead man to be resurrected to appear in his grave-clothes to vindicate him.

A year later, in 1927, the distinguished Polish art historian, Professor Mieczysław Gębarowicz, published a study on "the origin of the cult of Saint Stanisław" in which he seriously questioned the validity of Roosval's methodology, but more pertinently, he rejected the dating of the bas-reliefs at Tryde to the end of the twelfth century. He conceded one point to Roosval and Semkowicz, that the scenes depicted on the bas-reliefs refer to the cult of Saint Stanisław, but maintained that the baptismal font could not have been executed before the canonization bull of Pope Innocent IV in 1253. He reasoned that the bull would undoubtedly have mentioned the legend of the resurrection of Peter in the so-called Piotrawin incident. Gębarowicz further maintained that neither a cult of Saint Stanisław nor the legend of Piotrawin appear in the chronicle of Master Wincenty or the two *Lives* or the *Miracula*, but appear only after the beginning of the canonization process in the second half of the thirteenth century.

Gallus Anonymus and Master Wincenty give us contrasting accounts on the question of the "sentencing" of the bishop by means of a trial. Gallus wrote that the king "sentenced the bishop to dismemberment of limbs" [*obtruncatio membrorum*]. Master Wincenty's chronicle, on the other hand, with moral outrage, portrays the king's henchmen attacking the bishop in the church of Saint Stephen, then feeling remorse, and drawing back, whereupon the king himself "cast upon him his sacriligious hands." The two versions differ in two respects: Gallus seems to be saying that the bishop was sentenced, presumably by a court, but even this interpretation is open to debate; Master Wincenty mentions nothing about a trial. Second, Gallus's account implies that the king acted alone, whereas Kadłubek's account is clear, without the possibility of misunderstanding: that the king was not alone in committing the deed. Another scene in the Tryde bas-relief depicts a trial of a bishop. Semkowicz understood the scene to be a confirmation of the Anonymus's chronicle. Gębarowicz rejects the claim that the scene refers to the trial of Saint Stanisław. Instead, to him, the scene symbolically depicts martyrdom in general.

Professor Gębarowicz's contribution to the flowing debate on Saint Stanisław did not end with his criticism of the Semkowicz hypothesis. In 1937 he returned to the question again with a brilliant, though not unchallenged, paper on a well-known but misunderstood manuscript of Pope Paschal II (1099–1118). Professor Gębarowicz excitedly proclaimed to have found at long last that new evidence so eagerly sought by several generations of Polish scholars. Ironically, the document in question was known for a long time, but was rejected as not pertaining to Poland. It was variously attributed to Hungary, Sicily, Dalmatia, and Cologne. Undaunted by the fact that the original copy of Paschal's letter does not exist, nor that papal registers which listed the letter no longer exist, Gębarowicz launched into a masterly analysis of *Gesta pontificum romanorum* of Bosso, *camerarius* of Pope Hadrian IV (1154–1159) which contained lengthy excerpts of an undated letter to *Archiepiscopo Poloniensis*. Copyists in later centuries then changed *Poloniensis* into *Coloniensi* [Cologne], *Palermensi* [Palermo] or *Palmono* which would seem to be a personal name. The attribution to Dalmatia or Hungary is explained by the fact that at one point in the letter there is mention of a Hungarian prince.

Prescinding for the moment from the crucial question whether the letter is, in fact, addressed to the archbishop of Gniezno, what is the text of the letter as gleaned by Gębarowicz? He established to his own satisfaction that the letter was written by Pope Paschal II to Archbishop Marcin of Gniezno sometime between 1112 and 1115. The letter itself is in answer to a previous letter written to the pope by the archbishop. It seems that, in a letter accompanying the pallium sent to Archbishop Marcin, the pope demanded an oath of homage and fealty from him as a sign of the unity of the Church. Thereupon the archbishop, an appointee of the ruler, having taken an oath of fidelity to his lay lord, informed the pope of his refusal to take the oath as a violation of his previous oath, hence Paschal's reply.

Pope Paschal expressed *malum*—anger—at the state of the relations between the see of Peter and Poland (?). Written with a decidedly Gregorian reformist mentality, Paschal upbraids the archbishop for his wilful denial of the unity of the Church. Then comes the key question: "was it not your predecessor who, without the knowledge of the Roman pontiff, sentenced a bishop by a trial?" Then further, the pope adds: "what am I to say about the removal of bishops, which are carried out, among you, not through papal authority, but at the behest of the ruler?"

Gębarowicz and other scholars recognized this as an important, though not entirely conclusive, piece of evidence that Bishop Stanisław had, indeed, been sentenced by means of a trail, and apparently, a canonical process at which the archbishop presided. However, the pope's letter also seems to imply that it was usual for bishops to be removed "at the behest of the ruler," an uncanonical procedure which the Gregorian mind of Paschal II had rejected. The two questions posed by Paschal II, taken together, imply that a trial of the bishop was conducted, with the archbishop presiding, but that the trial had been held under duress by the ruler, therefore uncanonical and illegitimate from the Gregorian point of view.

If, indeed, the letter of Pope Paschal II does refer to Polish affairs, the archbishop in question who presided over the canonical process is unknown inasmuch as the eleventh century catalogue of the archbishops of Gniezno is lost. The letter itself throws greater light on the actual relations between the Church and the secular authority, and the weakness of ecclesiastical discipline in the early twelfth century than it does on the problem of the martyrdom of Saint Stanisław.

The Gębarowicz hypothesis must be regarded as a major effort, though not quite a breakthrough, in the quest for a solution to the mystery of Bishop Stanisław's death. His efforts do not enlighten us any further on the causes of the conflict which would have provoked the extreme measures of the king and led Gallus Anonymus to regard Bishop Stanisław as a traitor. Following the second World War, Polish scholars again returned to the vexing question: why did it happen? Among the several Polish scholars who resumed the debate were: Rev. Józef Umiński, Mme. Karolina Lanckorońska, and Professors Roman Grodecki, Karol Górski, and Witold Sawicki. The work of Professor Tadeusz Grudzinski, written from a Marxist perspective, is still unfinished, and therefore cannot here be considered. Mme. Lanckorońska's hypothesis has already been outlined and need not detain us here, other than to comment that it has not received wide support. Nor has the hypothesis of Karol Górski who tried to demonstrate that Saint Stanisław came from peasant ancestry. None of these scholars were able to produce any major contribution toward the solution of the mystery of the death of Saint Stanisław, their work suffering the weakness of all the earlier works.

The work of Witold Sawicki must be singled out among the postwar attempts at a new hypothesis. Taking advantage of the relatively new field of psycho-history, and adding philological insights into the problem, Sawicki has arrived at a new hypothesis which shifts the focus toward the *dramatis personae.* In a number of studies, Sawicki has attacked the Wojciechowski hypothesis and its variants on two grounds: first, that the term *traditor-traditio* may be interpreted as "rebel-rebellion"; second, paraphrasing the oft-repeated colloquialism that "he must have been demented to have done such a thing," Sawicki concluded that King Bolesław the Bold was psychologically ill, then marshals impressive evidence to prove his hypothesis. His hypothesis is succinctly stated thus: ". . . that Bolesław the Bold was stricken with an illness of a psychopathic type (an abnormal personality aberration, especially in feeling, impulse and will) with a psychotic character (an active and live disposition, changing moods, live and impulsive in his aggressive reactions, inclined toward conflicts and abuses of customs and alcoholism)."

If Professor Sawicki had not produced any new sources as evidence, at least he had introduced a new dimension into the debate which will be difficult to ignore any longer. Ironically, he begins his argument by defending the validity of the testimony of the chronicle of Master Wincenty. The chronicler was on very friendly terms with Duke Kazimierz the Just, son of Bolesław the Wrymouth, who was in turn a nephew of Bolesław the Bold. Therefore, Sawicki insisted, he received first-hand information about the tragic reign of Bolesław the Bold from his protector-friend, Kazimierz the Just, who was only a generation removed from his paternal grandfather, Bolesław the Bold. Such an argument depends too much on the element of probability, for it is just as probable that he did not receive credible information from his friend. It is not even certain, though quite probable, that a "Piast family tradition" had been forming and that Master Wincenty Kadłubek was both a receptor and propagator of that tradition. However, as Sawicki avers, there were certain stories which the chronicler would not report out of respect for his friend, Kazimierz the Just, and chose to present the more unpleasant ones metaphorically and analogically. Thus, at one point in the chronicle, Master Wincenty reaches into the First Book of Samuel, XVI, 14–23, where King David plays the lute in order to soothe the psychologically ill Saul, to advise that Bolesław the Bold ought to have learned from Saul how the sound of the lute cures the deranged soul.

Such evidence, although it provides a different perspective on the problem, obviously cannot stand alone. Sawicki then reaches into the family background of Bolesław the Bold to buttress the cryptic testimony of Master Wincenty. From various sources, mainly of German provenance, Sawicki culls a story of psychological illness in Bolesław the Bold's family on the side of his maternal grandmother, Rycheza. Two brothers of Rycheza, Herman, palatine of Lorraine, and Conrad, margrave of Carinthia, were psychologically ill.

Sawicki then interprets two incidents from the chronicle of Gallus Anonymus to prove the king's demented condition: his relations with Iziaslav of Kiev (1068) and King Ladislaus of Hungary (1079). In both incidents, the king exhibited a lack of self-control and arrogance. After having aided Iziaslav to regain his throne in Kiev, Bolesław the Bold was asked to participate in a ceremony sealing the friendship between the two warriors on horseback. Instead of dismounting himself and offering his ally a kiss of peace and friendship, the Polish king unaccountably remained mounted and pulled his host's beard instead, whereupon Iziaslav drove Bolesław out of Kiev, killing many Poles.

The second incident cited by Sawicki refers to Bolesław the Bold's entry into exile in Hungary, again depicted by Gallus Anonymus. As the exile approached the Hungarian king, courtesy and friendship required that he again dismount in deference to an equal who had already dismounted, awaiting his cousin's arrival. Instead, Bolesław displayed uncommon arrogance to the very person who was offering him asylum by his refusal to dismount and greet his benefactor. The results of the first incident weakened the Polish king in Ruthenia, the second lost him a friend and ally in Hungary and hastened his death.

Such behavior, Sawicki reasons, alarmed the king's council and the royal guard who had frequently witnessed their king's cruel and rapacious demeanor. Moreover, a coalition of enemies, led by the Ruthenian and Czech kings, surrounded Poland, suggesting to the king's advisors the necessity of removing the irresponsible Bolesław as illegitimate because he constituted a danger to the monarchy itself. Thus, the plot which Wojciechowski had charged the Bishop of Kraków with having been a participant, in alliance with Poland's enemies was, according to Sawicki, a plot to save the monarchy of the Piasts from an irresponsible king, therefore a purely internal matter.

But, the term *traditor* still had to be confronted. It is Sawicki's contention that the term *traditor* in the medieval Latin was understood in a dual sense. It could mean "traitor," as Wojciechowski understood it, following Du Cange. It was also used as "rebel," i.e. illegal opposition to legal authority. Here, a survey of the manner in which the term was used in the period in question strengthens such a contention of dual use. Indeed, according to Sawicki, Gallus Anonymus himself, a few pages earlier in his chronicle used the term *traditor* to describe those who exiled Rycheza, Bolesław the Bold's grandmother, to Germany, *propter invidiam*—"because of jealousy." Pope Gregory VII was also declared a *traditor regni* by a synod of bishops allied to his adversary, Emperor Henry IV. This, in fact, was a subjective judgment by elements who did not agree with Gregory's policies toward the Church in Germany. Thus, in the latter case, Gregory was a *traditor*, not because he allied himself illegally with external enemies, but because he entered an internal conflict on the side of rebels against the emperor.

The Sawicki hypothesis attacks the Wojciechowski hypothesis at its most vital point. If Saint Stanisław became part of a plot to remove the king from his throne because of misrule and tyranny, a perfectly legal act, why did Gallus Anonymus condemn the bishop as having committed a sin? Was the Anonymus chronicler subjectively expressing the feeling of the Piast family whose servant he was that, no matter what the circumstances were, Saint Stanisław was not justified in joining a plot against the king's rule, thus "one sin was committed over another sin?"

The Sawicki hypothesis still needs greater refinement to be accepted, but it is at this moment a plausible explanation of those "other matters" which so deeply affected Pope Gregory VII in 1075. These "other matters" probably led to the death of the Bishop of Kraków, Stanisław of Szczepanów, then to the crisis of the Piast dynasty—loss of the royal crown, eventually loss of unity because of subdivision—and finally to the cult of Saint Stanisław together with the condemnation of King Bolesław II the Bold, whose reign had begun so auspiciously and ended so tragically.

The cult of Saint Stanisław, nurtured throughout the thirteenth century, abetted by the canonization process begun under Pope Innocent IV, became in the succeeding centuries an "official" national version of a martyred saint falling victim to royal tyranny and brutality, an authentic national hero-saint, indeed the patron saint of Polish Catholicism. It was the misfortune of the late Professor Wojciechowski to have upset that traditional version of the martyred saint, thus contributing to the polarization of Polish scholarship. Aware of this, he tried to defend himself by claiming that his hypothesis did not foreclose the issue, for new evidence would undoubtedly be found. Moreover, as for the continued existence of a cult in veneration of the martyred bishop, there need be no fear, for it has existed "for six and a half centuries, and has merged with the tradition of the nation to such an extent that it can no longer disappear."

Professor Wojciechowski deserved better. He opened up a serious and wide-ranging discussion of an historical problem which continued to wallow in hagiography. Though Professor Wojciechowski was perhaps prematurely confident in his conclusion that "the case of Saint Stanisław, according to my perception of the matter, is lost," based on the availability of the sources then available, those interpreters of the problem who followed him were always conscious of the fact that it was he who had clearly presented to them the state of the question.

Though the problems raised by Wojciechowski have not been resolved, and the life and death of Saint Stanisław still remains a mystery, it has not been a fruitless exercise in hypothetical reasoning. A new perspective has been opened on the relations between king and bishop; various issues of great historical importance related to the conflict between king and bishop have received the attention of a new post-war generation of Polish scholars.

On the nine hundredth anniversary of the death of Saint Stanisław, bishop and martyr, the hope is that hypothesis will become theory.

DANIEL S. BUCZEK

Fairfield, Connecticut
February 28, 1979

KRAKÓW—Through the Centuries

PROLOGUE

IN THE AUTUMN of 1491, there arrived in the city Saint Stanisław had known, a young man who was eventually to be counted as another among Kraków's numerous famous sons. "Nicholas, the son of Nicholas of Toruń" inscribed himself in the registrar's records of the university, omitting thereby the Latinized form of his family name—Copernicus, Kopernik in Polish—by which he is best known today. He would have approached the city where he was to spend three, and possibly four, years in study from the northeast. His route would either have brought him up the Wisła (Vistula), the mystic river that has succored Poland throughout the vicissitudes of its more than ten centuries of history, or taken him overland through the wild highlands of the Swiety Krzyz (Holy Cross) mountains. In either case, upon approach he would have had spread before him a panorama of the city similar to that presented to us in the rather stylized woodcut which Hartmann Schedel included in his *Nuremberg Chronicle* of 1493. From a height outside Kraków he, and by extension we with him, could see a city which was the largest in the kingdom, a royal, ecclesiastical, and an intellectual center which one of the popes of the fifteenth century, Pius II, described as "a city adorned by the study of letters."

The Kraków which Copernicus would have seen, and which we see before us in Schedel's print, was surrounded completely by wall and encircled by a moat and the river. Outside the fortifications, suburbs are visible; inside, the city presents a view of prosperous burgher houses, many impressive church towers, and a great central square with its town hall and merchant emporium. The university itself is nearly invisible, tucked off in one quarter of the city. Its buildings face inward upon its own life, and from the outside there is little hint given that in importance it is the equal of the other features which strike the eye. In the distance looms the acropolis of Wawel hill, dominated by its independent fortifications, by the royal castle, and by the cathedral of Saint Wacław, which is the seat of the Bishop of Kraków. Having paused to view, Copernicus would have entered Kraków to begin his university career. He joined himself thereby to the life of the parts he had seen: a city whose multiple dimensions were social and urban, economic, religious, political, and intellectual. It was the city of Saint Stanisław, but its development had in many respects made it a different city from that which the eleventh century bishop had known; it was also a city whose dynamic evolution after Copernicus has maintained it as a vital center. Let us enter that city with him. The pages which follow trace some of the important developments in the history of Kraków that bear upon the lives of the famous sons of which it boasts.

FROM THE SETTLEMENT TO THE ERA OF STANISŁAW

In the dim mists of pre-history, the beginnings of the city of Kraków are to be found. On the upper course of the Wisław River there lived one of the several Slavonic tribes which eventually formed the Polish state. This group was the Wiślanie, and it was they who during the eighth and ninth centuries first chose a site commanding the river as their stronghold. That they were not the first to live in this region is shown by the variety of archaeological finds which antedate A.D. 600. Potsherds, weapons, stones and metal tools, and even coins attest to the succession of peoples who took up residence upon the several hills in this area. But the Wiślanie were apparently the first to fortify the acropolis which became known as Wawel hill and to organize the region around under their control. The slow, gradual nature of this process, which was accompanied by their strengthening of the military strongpoint was in reality a good deal more prosaic than the legends which have come down to us about the founding of Kraków.

According to the twelfth century chronicler, Bishop Wincenty Kadłubek of Kraków, who was repeating stories that were by then centuries old (and which were repeated by Schedel in his *Chronicle*), the region around the eventual city was being terrorized by a dragon which lived in a cave beneath the hill. The local ruler offered his daughter's hand in marriage and a share of the rule to anyone who could kill the beast. An enterprising young man named Krak eventually accomplished the deed by throwing a sheep-skin, stuffed with phosphorous, into the dragon's lair. The beast swallowed the ruse whole, and the next time it drank from the Wisła, it went up in smoke. Krak established his residence on the hill, and the town took its name from him. If we disregard the legendary aspects of this tale, one important point is nevertheless reflected in the story: the early identification of Kraków and Wawel. The city developed in conjunction with the acropolis, not separate from it. Even in subsequent centuries, when there was also settlement on the plain beneath Wawel, the association of both geographical areas was strong. Kraków was a single entity, not a commercial and princely bifurcation, as was true of many towns in Europe.

The domination that the Wiślanie established was a precarious one and did not last. The Great Moravian Empire, which grew up in the ninth century in the central part of present day Czechoslovakia, extended its control over the region of Kraków and may even have introduced Christianity there in the form of the Slavonic rite established earlier in Moravia through the missionary activity of Saints Cyril and Methodius. After the Moravian Empire was destroyed by the Magyars (Hungarians) in the late ninth and early tenth centuries, the region of Kraków was again autonomous under the Wiślanie. But the princes of Bohemia soon expanded their control into the area, and it was not until the end of the tenth century that Duke Mieszko I, the leader of the

Polanie tribe from the region of Gniezno and Poznań in central Poland, succeeded in driving the Bohemians out and uniting his tribe and the Wiślanie into the Polish state. When he converted to Catholic Christianity in the 960's, he bound Poland's culture and history forever to the Latin west.

By that time, Kraków had become an important settlement. The peripatetic Arab-speaking Jew, Ibrahim-ibn-Jakub, writing in the mid-tenth century, tells us that it was a significant trading point on the commercial route running from Kiev through Prague to Regensburg. Among the goods carried on this route were salt, slaves, and amber. Given this commercial importance, it is not surprising that we should find a thriving, if small, settlement in tenth century Kraków. Atop Wawel there was a wooden fortress, perhaps with a single stone tower (remnants of which have been discovered in this century), which was the residence of the prince. This was complemented by wooden structures for the princely retainers and by other buildings housing people who conducted trade and provided such products as the court needed (weapons, in particular). Also on the hill was the site of the earliest church in Kraków. Dedicated to Saint Mary (in later years rededicated to Saints Felix and Adauctus), this small stone structure, of which only fragments remain today, was built in the form of a rotunda. Its very form—a compact fortress—reminds us of the close association between the ruler and the religion at this time. In normal circumstances, churches were private chapels belonging to the owner of the military strong point, and the Polish word for a church (*kościół*) is etymologically derived from the Latin for burg or fortress (*castellum*). To the west of Wawel, about one and one-half kilometers up the Wisła, another early church was located. Atop Saint Bronisława's hill, the church of the Holy Savior was also built of stone and served a small community there. Although part of the city now, throughout the middle ages this area remained separate from Kraków proper. Thus in the century when

Poland entered upon the stage of history—if by this one means that its presence was recorded in the writings of the time—Kraków was of sufficient importance that when the Emperor Otto III visited Gniezno in the year 1000, the city was officially recognized as one of the bishoprics of the Polish church, thus confirming a status which had existed for a generation. In subsequent years, Kraków grew and developed into something which was much more complex by the time of Saint Stanisław.

The story of the life and death of the martyred bishop have been told elsewhere by chronicler Hartmann Schedel and by historian D. S. Buczek. Here the focus is upon the city in his time. One of the most striking differences between the end of the tenth century and the end of the eleventh century was the physical growth of Kraków. No longer was there a settlement only atop Wawel. A marketplace, established on the plain below about three-quarters of a kilometer away, served as the center of the town's growing commercial activity, both the handling and the manufacture of goods. This center attracted increasing numbers of residents, and with their arrival additional churches were built. In addition, there were settlements growing up in sections that would ultimately become suburbs of Kraków. The most striking changes, however, had come at Wawel itself and had come in conjunction with the events of the eleventh century.

Although it was as a Polish duke that Bolesław the Brave had greeted the emperor at Gniezno in 1000, his title had changed by his death. Taking advantage of weaknesses within Germany, Bolesław had assumed the royal crown in 1025. Although not all Polish rulers were henceforth to be kings, the existence of a Kingdom of Poland was to be a constant and crucial element in Polish unity for the next centuries. To symbolize this new status, which had been foreshadowed by successful wars against the Empire, Bohemia, and Kiev, Bolesław began the construction of a cathedral on Wawel. Named in honor of the martyred Bohemian Duke Václav (d. 929—in Polish: Wacław), this basilican structure was built of sandstone and had three naves, making it an impressive building at this time. It was largely destroyed not long after it was completed, and its fate is symbolic of that of the country after Bolesław's death.

Internal weaknesses within the structure of the Polish monarchy allowed foreigners and local princes to range at will in Poland in the 1030's and 1040's. The Bohemians attacked Poland in this period and sacked Kraków and Gniezno, carrying off many valuable treasures and religious relics. Included among the latter were the remains of Saint Wojciech (Adalbert), a friend of Bolesław I who had died while trying to convert the Prussians in 999. He eventually had a small church built to his memory in the main part of Kraków. Only with some difficulties were Poland's problems overcome and a measure of unity re-established by King Kazimierz (Casimir) (1034–1058), who quite properly was surnamed Odnowiciel, ''The Restorer.'' He rebuilt towns and churches, reorganized and invigorated the Polish clergy, and revived monastic life (he himself had been educated in a monastery). This last activity included the foundation of the great Benedictine monastery at Tuniec, a few kilometers up the Wisła from Kraków.

One of the most significant acts of King Kazimierz was that he transferred the capital to Kraków. This promoted what had been merely a town, albeit an important one, into a royal metropolis. Henceforth Kraków was, as the twelfth century chronicler put it, ''the city and seat of the king,'' and the place ''where the Polish crown has been since antiquity'' (an obvious, if understandable, exaggeration). By the same measure, the Bishop of Kraków became by virtue of his proximity to the royal seat a figure of great importance and moment. That this did not always have positive results is clear from the reign of Bolesław the Bold, who succeeded Kazimierz in 1058. The fate of Stanisław at Bolesław's hands came in part from his close association with the political issues at the court.

ROMANESQUE KRAKÓW AND THE EARLY GOTHIC PERIOD

Władysław Herman, the weak and pliant younger brother of Bolesław, became ruler following the murder of Stanisław. Despite his shortcomings, he made his mark upon Kraków, for it was he who initiated the building of a large Romanesque-style cathedral on Wawel. Containing three naves, its construction continued until the mid-twelfth century. Of this splendid structure, whose construction and the considerable expenses connected with it reflect the growing economic vitality of Kraków, there remain today only the crypt, named in honor of Saint Leonard, fragments of walls incorporated into later remodeling, and a bell tower. At about the same time, two other churches were erected which are extant today. One was the monumental Saint Andrzej's (Andrew), which for a time constituted the royal court's collegiate church. This building, with three naves and two towers, is today one of the finest examples of the Romanesque style in Poland and still plays an important role in the ecclesiastical life of the city. Its fortress-like structure enabled it to withstand successfully the tribulations which were visited upon Kraków in subsequent years. The second church built in this period was the aforementioned Saint Wojciech's, which, despite many intervening alterations, still shows traces of the granite and limestone used in its original construction. In this time, it lay on the western periphery of the settlement that had grown up around the market place.

These positive developments were counterbalanced by political dislocations. Władysław Herman had not assumed the royal title, and during his lifetime his rule was challenged by many other dukes. Following the death of his son Bolesław Krzywousty (the Wrymouth) in 1138, the Kingdom of Poland was divided up into several territorial parts. For the next century and a half, Poland was riven by particularism and petty factionalism which destroyed the unity of the state. Although all the dukes of the area belonged to the family of the ruling dynasty, the Piast family, they vied inconclusively for predominance. Their conflicting ambitions caused political order and stability to degenerate into near anarchy. As a symbol of this situation, in the mid-thirteenth century Poland was visited by the scourge of the Mongols, whom contemporaries viewed as divine judgement upon their own sins. The Mongol attack fell particularly severely upon Kraków.

Even though this invasion was only a diversionary arm of the main force, the heirs of those who fell victim to the looting and burning of these Tatar soldiers long remembered the dreadful year of 1241; and the impression these fast-riding horsemen left was one which menaced the Polish mind for generations. When the Mongols came to Kraków, they found a settlement only partially protected by earthworks and a wooden palisade. It was easy for them to destroy and burn the wooden houses and buildings which had grown up along the routes to the market and Wawel. According to the legend still told in the city, a story transmitted to the English-speaking world in the charming children's book by Eric Kelly, *The Trumpeter of Kraków*, the inhabitants were given brief warning of the attack. A lookout atop Saint Mary's church blew the alarm, but his signal was tragically broken off by the impact of a Mongol arrow. (The *hejnał*, which someone blows hourly to the four winds in contemporary Kraków, stops abruptly before the end of the bugle call, reminding all who hear it of this event long ago.) Unable to defend the city, the citizens retreated to whatever shelter they could individually find. For many it was not enough. The Mongols left behind them a town in which half the population was dead and where most of the structures smoldered in ruins. Only stone buildings survived. The promising early history of Kraków seemed to have come to an end. Instead, this disaster served as a beginning; a more prosperous and spectacular city arose, Phoenix-like, from the ashes.

The new Kraków received a formal charter of location based on western models from a local duke in 1257, thus establishing its corporate autonomy as an urban center. Unlike the old settlement, which had grown haphazardly through the generations, this city was from the beginning a planned community. A new market square was established on the western outskirts of the Romanesque settlement. Unusually large by medieval standards, it measured nearly 200 meters on a side. On it were eventually built a city hall, a large cloth hall, with numerous stalls for merchants, and the municipal scale. Thus the physical focus of the town clearly reflected the commercial character of the city. The city streets were plotted on a grid, so they were straight and regular. Around the settlement a wall and towers were begun. These eventually defined a roughly oval form for the city, with the southern half narrowing slightly to adjoin the fortified acropolis of Wawel. At its greatest physical extent, it stretched some 800 by 600 meters. Within this area the previous stone structures that had been largely self-contained, such as the church of Saint Andrezej, were incorporated into the city. Outside the walls, suburban settlements began to grow up, one in Kleparz to the north, another to the south across an arm of the Wisła. Even the water courses which surrounded the city were planned, for in the wake of the relocation of 1257, efforts were made to channel the Wisła and the smaller Rudawa River. In the generations following the disaster of 1241, despite several further Mongol attacks of lesser severity, medieval Kraków gradually took form.

As Kraków grew, a unified Polish state also developed apace. This is symbolized by the testimony given in the mid-thirteenth century by the author of a life of Saint Stanisław. He reported that in conjunction with the canonization process the tomb of the martyred bishop had been opened. In it the dismembered corpse had been found to be miraculously knit together into a whole. This was taken as a harbinger of eventual Polish unity. The actual process of political unification was considerably more complicated, and required nearly three-quarters of a century after the canonization of the saint. On the eve of the fourteenth century, inspired by a Polish Church which had never been disunited, stimulated by the increasing cohesion of the Polish gentry, catalyzed by a growing territorial threat from abroad, supported by the commercial interests of the towns, particularly Kraków, and led vigorously by a series of ambitious and powerful Piast dukes, a movement toward political unification emerged. It was finally accomplished permanently by Władysław I Łokietek, and the city of Kraków was the focus of the process. Whoever held it had taken a long step toward ultimate victory.

Łokietek first became Duke of Kraków in 1289, but soon lost the city in the political turmoil which surrounded attempts by others to establish Polish unity. Not until 1306 was he able to recover the city. Then he was faced with the hostility of the Bishop of Kraków, an ambitious duke from Śląsk (Silesia) and the *advocatus* (an independent civil administrator) of Kraków. These fomented rebellion in 1311, and for some days they besieged him, his wife, and infant son Kazimierz in the fortress on Wawel. Eventually troops loyal to Łokietek arrived, and the revolt was crushed. The dissidents had been chiefly drawn from the German community which had become important in Kraków's civic and commercial life, and an arbitrary test was devised by Łokietek's supporters to determine who was loyal to him. All those suspected were questioned. Every one who could successfully demonstrate his Polishness by correctly pronouncing *soczowycza, koło, myelye młyn* was spared; the others were executed. Firmly established in Kraków, Łokietek was gradually able to extend his dominance over several other Polish territories. He failed only in Śląsk, where Bohemian influence was strong, and in Pomerania (Pomorze), which had been comquered by the Knights of the Teutonic Order, the rulers of Prussia. Nevertheless, his achievements were sufficient to gain papal support for his coronation. On Sunday 20 January 1320, the Archbishop of Gniezno placed the crown of a reunited Poland upon his head in the cathedral of Kraków that Władysław Herman had begun in the eleventh century. This coronation marked the beginning of the greatest period in the history of Kraków, the two and one-half centuries of the last Piasts and the Jagiellonian kings.

THE ROYAL CAPITAL UNDER THE LAST PIASTS

Władysław Łokietek and his successor, Kazimierz III Wielki (Casimir the Great), brought great changes to Kraków, and their reigns saw important developments in all aspects of the city's life. Both men were great builders, though the son overshadowed the father in this respect. (The fifteenth century historian Jan Długosz, consciously echoing the Roman historian Livy, wrote about Kazimierz that "he found a Poland built of wood and left one built of stone.") Under Łokietek's patronage, the Bishop of Kraków began the rebuilding of the cathedral of Saint Wacław. The Romanesque structure was largely replaced with a Gothic one, which is built in the characteristic Polish style without flying buttresses. In this building, as in others elsewhere in the country, the vaults are born by external supports which are flush with the walls and by internal strengthening on the aisle side of the piers. The reconstruction of the cathedral was completed during the reign of Kazimierz, and it remains essentially unchanged today except for the additions to be mentioned below.

The last two Piasts also built a new royal castle on Wawel. A fire in 1306 had destroyed the earlier home of the dukes of Kraków, so Łokietek began the construction of a new brick fortress. Kazimierz added to this and strengthened the fortifications on the hill, making the heights increasingly defensible. These walls, and those of the city below, were tested in the 1340's when the blind king of Bohemia, John of Luxemburg, invaded Poland and besieged Kraków. Kazimierz offered to fight a duel with John in order to determine the outcome of the conflict without further warfare, but he changed his mind when John accepted on the condition that Kazimierz be given the same visual handicap he had.

Two other important architectural transformations in the city were initiated during the rule of the last Piasts and encouraged by them. The wooden structure which had long served the cloth merchants of the city was replaced by a magnificent brick hall, which occupied the center of the market square. Built in the Gothic style (though it has today sixteenth and seventeenth century additions), this building is one of the finest examples of secular architecture extant from the late middle ages. The wealth of the great merchants who used this structure was, in part, applied to another great building project in this period. The parish church of Saint Mary's, which faces the market square on the northeast corner, was transformed into a Gothic building that is remarkable for its extreme height-to-width ratio. If the cathedral atop Wawel was a fitting home for the ecclesiastical aristocracy of Kraków, symbolizing its wealth and power, and if the castle finally befit the royal dignity, the church of Saint Mary served as an equally appropriate monument to the achievements and affluence of the urban patriciate.

In addition to the specific buildings mentioned above (which are merely representative of all that was accomplished in Kraków during Łokietek's and Kazimierz's time), the city was changed also by the further development of its suburbs. To the east and west, in Wesoła and Garbary, increased settlement may be noted in this period. The section of Stradom, lying at the foot of the southern slope of Wawel, was annexed to the city together with its armories and other manufacturing activities. But the most important suburb was one which became a city in its own right in this period. Across the Wisła, south of the city of Kraków, lay a settlement which Kazimierz incorporated in 1335, modestly naming it after himself: Kazimierz. Although never equal in size to Kraków—the capital may have had a population of 12,000 in Kazimierz's time, the city of Kazimierz probably had only about 1500 inhabitants—this new city was in some respects a modest economic challenge to the commercial and industrial position of Kraków. One of the most important aspects of the city's history, however, is that it became increasingly the home of Jews who moved to Poland. Kazimierz the Great showed great religious tolerance to all, including the so-called "schismatics" of Greek and Armenian Orthodoxy who inhabited the lands he conquered to the east. But his protection of the Jews was especially marked, and he granted them wide ranging privileges and promised to ensure their rights in Poland. (Some contemporaries attributed this royal attitude to the fact that Kazimierz supposedly had a Jewish mistress, a certain Esterka, who bore him children.) Since this came at a time when other European states were increasingly hostile to the Jews, they found a home which welcomed them in Poland. Although Kraków also had a Jewish area, Kazimierz was to become the focus of the Jewish settlement in subsequent generations. By the end of the fourteenth century there was a substantial brick synagogue in the Gothic style in Kazimierz.

During the reign of Kazimierz from 1333 to 1370, Kraków was witness to many dramatic moments. One of particular importance came in 1364, with the Congress of Kraków. It was this event which symbolized the emergence of Poland as an important central European power and Kraków as one of the leading capitals of the day. A century before, the country had been riven by particularism and threatened by numerous foreign foes; the city had barely begun the recovery from the Mongol attack. Now it was the scene of the most glittering international meeting of the century. This "grand gathering," as the contemporary chronicler and royal Vice-chancellor Janko of Czarnków called it, was held at the request of Emperor Charles IV to discuss a regional response to the growing threat which the Ottoman Turks posed to the southern and eastern frontiers of Christendom. In addition to the emperor and Kazimierz, there were the kings of Bohemia, Hungary, Denmark, and Cyprus who attended. They were joined by half-a-dozen dukes and a host of lesser princes. The rulers were Kazimierz's guests in the royal castle, while the others found lodging in the city. Kazimierz liberally distributed gifts to his guests, numerous games and tourneys were held, and Nicholas Wierzynek, a city councillor and reputedly the richest man in Kraków, sumptuously entertained the whole congress in his private quarters on the central market square. (The building is still there, and the tradition of Wierzynek's hospitality has been continued in the fine contemporary restaurant that has been established in it.) For nearly three weeks the guests enjoyed themselves and passed the time amid the spectacular results of the building which had been done in Kraków during the reigns of the last Piasts. Although the formal business of the congress led to no concrete action, the meeting was not without its highlights. Kazimierz used it as the occasion for celebrating one of the most important accomplishments of his reign, the founding of a university.

During his time, the cultural evolution of Poland had proceeded sufficiently to support such an institution, and the needs of Polish society made its establishment increasingly imperative. Within the kingdom there was a flourishing network of schools which could prepare students, there were important libraries, especially at the cathedral of Saint Wacław and Saint Mary's church in Kraków, whose contents could support instruction, and there were men trained in western universities who could serve as faculty. The elaboration of both secular and ecclesiastical institutions of governance, the king's preparation of a codification of Polish law, and his establishment of new law courts: all these required men with university training.

As early as 1351, in the aftermath of Charles IV's foundation of the University of Prague, Kazimierz had sent one of his most trusted advisors to Italy to investigate the legal studies there. Other affairs of state had intervened, however, and it was not until 1362 that he attempted to arrange for a similar school in Poland, to be established in Kazimierz. (He even began the building of a university complex which, according to Długosz, was "a thousand paces square." The basement vaults of these buildings are still extant.) Opposition from the city council of Kraków and the Bishop of Kraków caused him to change his mind about location, and in 1363 he sent a delegation to the pope to request approval for a university in Kraków. This was given, and on 12 May 1364 Kazimierz issued a royal charter erecting the university and providing for one chair in arts, two in medicine, three in canon law, and five in civil law, the professor for each to be paid out of the income from the royal salt monopoly. To this university, Kazimierz invited both natives and foreigners, with the hope that they "might endeavor to obtain the pearl of knowledge." This same day, the city council of Kraków issued a charter listing the extensive privileges and immunities it was granting to the new school. Thus when the Congress of Kraków assembled in that summer, its host was able to celebrate an important cultural advance.

Despite these ambitious beginnings the school experienced difficulties from the start. Faculty were difficult to attract, too few students enrolled, and the royal patron was not followed after his death by anyone else who supported the school. It functioned for a while, graduating some students, then sank into decrepitude. Sometime after the early 1370's it ceased to function. Only the tradition and the ideal remained to inspire a later revival in a Kraków much changed and a city under a new dynasty.

The end of the Piast dynasty came in the late fall of 1370. Kazimierz had fallen from a horse on a hunt in central Poland, and while recovering from the injury suffered at that time, he developed pneumonia. Brought back to Kraków by a retinue that increasingly resembled a cortege, the king died in the royal castle about sunrise on 5 November. He was buried in the cathedral amidst ceremonies in which the princes, prelates, and populace of Poland mourned so greatly that Janko of Czarnków reported it was "impossible for the human tongue to describe the extent of the clamor, lamentation, and outcries." Kazimierz was the only Polish king to be surnamed "the Great." The marble monument and sarcophagus erected later in the cathedral is one of the most magnificent of Kraków's artistic glories. Great as was his reign, however, it was but the prelude to the greatness of his capital in the generations to come.

JAGIELLONIAN KRAKÓW

Kazimierz died without male heir and was succeeded by his nephew, King Louis of Hungary. His unhappy twelve year rule over Poland was marked by factional strife and political drift. Janko of Czarnków later wrote bitterly that "at the time of that king there was neither stability nor justice in the Kingdom of Poland." Louis also had no male heir, and in 1384 (after a two-year interregnum) the Polish magnates accepted his younger daughter Jadwiga as their ruler. That same year she was crowned king (because the Poles refused to be ruled by a queen and because this was a way to forestall her future husband from claiming the same title). In the next, the magnates arranged for her to be married to the Grand Prince of pagan Lithuania. This mature and experienced ruler became a convert, Polonized his given name to Jagiełło, and took the additional Christian name Władysław. He outlived Jadwiga, who died childless at the age of twenty-six in 1399, by thirty-five years and by virtue of a fruitful later marriage thus became the founder of the Jagiellonian dynasty which ruled Poland and Lithuania jointly until its own extinction in 1572. In these years, Kraków flourished.

By the end of the fifteenth century it was completely encircled by a stone wall which averaged ten meters in height. Along its course were placed more than a dozen towers, which both strengthened the wall and provided a position for lookout and defense. The city was entered through one of the seven great gates which pierced the walls. The municipal system of fortifications was completed late in the century (1495–1498), by the construction of a brick barbican, completely surrounded by a wide moat. Not yet built when Copernicus arrived or when Schedel commissioned the woodcut of Kraków for the *Nuremburg Chronicle*, it stood in front of the Saint Florian's gate, which is visible to us in the illustration in the lower right corner. Around the city there ran a moat, fashioned by channeling the Rudawa. This waterway, which also served to drive the mills of the city, was complete by 1506. Above the city, on Wawel, the early Jagiellonians extended the fortifications by building additional towers and enclosing the entire acropolis within walls. They also enlarged the royal castle slightly, while on the side overlooking the city they constructed a massive palatium and tower, which is picturesquely called "the hen's foot."

On the town square, the city hall received an upper story and tower, the single spire of Saint Mary's was raised in height and a second tower added in this period, and the so-called "Rich Men's Shop" was built parallel to the earlier cloth hall in order to provide a special site for wealthy merchants to handle cloth and other costly goods. Surrounding the square were the two and three story homes of affluent merchants and other members of the urban patriciate. Although some of these houses were constructed of stone or brick, even at the end of the century many were still wooden. The cumulative effect of the central square was thus of a municipal center on a grand scale, reflecting the prosperity of the city. By the mid-sixteenth century, there were approximately 18,000 inhabitants in the city, with another 5000 living in Kazimierz and some 2000 in Kleparz. When those who were not counted in the data from which the above figures are derived (i.e., Jews and other suburban residents) are included, the population of the urban area as a whole was probably between 28,000 and 30,000.

Any description of the city in the late fifteenth and early sixteenth century would not be complete without mentioning that Kraków was also a center of production. The present day pollution problems of the city were foreshadowed in this time by the foundry just outside Kraków of the Thurzon family, who had come originally from Hungary. There, copper, gold, and silver were smelted, and a contemporary remarked that the area "looked like Mt. Etna, with furnaces burning full of . . . [metals] . . . being joined in the fire." In addition, there were iron foundries in the area, and the processing of lead was a lucrative business.

The physical change and economic development sketched above is the background against which it is possible to see Gothic Kraków transformed into a Renaissance city. In the market square, the most visible manifestation of this was the attic which was added to the cloth hall and the graceful arches of the arcades which were constructed alongside it. Elsewhere, colored "sgrafitto" ornamentation was added to many of the private homes, and gothic windows were replaced with newer styles. Nowhere, however, is the Renaissance style more evident than on Wawel itself. Zygmunt I Stary (Sigismund the Old), who ruled from 1506 to 1548, had not yet become king when fire destroyed part of the old castle. He determined to rebuild it in the new style, whose harbingers can be observed in other Cracovian buildings (particularly the *Collegium Maius*, which we shall discuss below). These tastes were reinforced early in his reign when he married Bona Sforza, a Milanese princess who brought to Poland a host of Italian architects and stylemakers in her entourage. The resultant reconstruction of the royal residence, carried out by both Polish and Italian masters, blends Renaissance and Gothic elements in a variety of ways. The huge quadrangle of the inner court (50 by 65 meters) is defined by porches which rise above it in three levels. The first two of these are enclosed in graceful Italian-ate arches, while the top-most one is supported by columns whose height is reminiscent of Gothic slimness. The four wings of the building are joined by towers, while inside the series of chambers are lit through post-and-lintel windows and decorated with the luxuries and comforts that befitted a Renaissance prince. Among these are the magnificent Flemish tapestries which Zygmunt's successor, Zygmunt II August (Sigismund Augustus), commissioned from Arras and elsewhere. What had been a castle had become a palace, and the last Jagiellonians lived in a residence which even the imperial comforts of the Habsburgs did not surpass.

Nor was it only the palace on Wawel which felt the transforming touch of Renaissance taste. The cathedral too received significant alterations. Chief among these were the several chapels which were added to the church. The most important is the Zygmunt Chapel, a square mausoleum for the sarcophaguses of the last two Jagiellonians. This nearly cubical space is surmounted by an octagonal drum that is pierced with round windows. It in turn is topped by a magnificent dome with gilt overlay. The interior is full of sculptural detail, while the con-trast created by the native green sandstone and red Hungarian marble used in the chapel presents the viewer with an image of both splendor and harmony. With justice has this structure, built by Bartolomeo Berecci between 1519 and 1531, been called by a German art historian "the gem of Renaissance style north of the Alps."

That the older traditions were not without vitality, however, is shown by the completion in Kraków of a masterpiece of Gothic sculp-ture in the late fifteenth century. The woodcarver Wit Stwosz worked in Kraków for several years in this time, before returning to the Vischer atelier in Nuremberg. His bronze epitaph plate for the Italian humanist known as Callimachus hangs in the Dominican church, and his sarco-phagus in red and white marble for King Kazimierz IV Jagiellończyk

(Casimir the Jagiellonian, d. 1492) is among the greatest treasures of Saint Wacław's cathedral. But his masterpiece was the polychromed wood altar he carved between 1477 and 1489 for Saint Mary's church. This ten meter high work depicts, in panels on both the inside and outside of its massive double wings, stories from the Old Testament and from the life of Christ. The chief theme of the altar, however, is the Virgin Mary, and it is she who dominates the larger-than-life-size figures in the central grouping. Her lyrical grace, the expressive and plastic qualities of Stwosz's carving, the dramatic elements reflected in the group scenes, and the realistic representations mark this altar as one of the highest achievements of the late Gothic style.

Thus the cultural tradition of Kraków in the time of the Jagiellon-ians was a combination of the old and the new. Nowhere is this more clearly seen than in the institution which was the central pearl in the crown of the city's reputation, the restored University of Kraków. It was Władysław II Jagiełło who in 1400 refounded the school. Unlike its Casimiran predecessor, which had been organized on the model of Bologna, this university took Paris as its example. It was therefore the professors who chose the administration. In addition, the curriculum included the faculty of theology, which had been missing from the earlier school. Unlike the homeless Piast foundation, which held classes in churches, the castle, and private quarters, the Jagiellonian creation was given a building by the king. This became, after numerous additions and remodelings in the course of the century, a self-contained collegiate quadrangle (known then, as now, as the *Collegium Maius*) in which lectures were held and the faculty housed. When much of the building was gutted by fire in the 1490's, the faculty met to agree on what repairs should be made. After "much mature deliberation" (so the minutes of that meeting tell us), it was decided to rebuild "in as beautiful form as possible." The eventual result of that reconstruction provided an interior courtyard which is fully in harmony with some of the architectural ideals being evolved in Renaissance Italy. The university thus is one of the early influences in Polish society of this new taste.

The *Collegium Maius* was not the only building of the school. Founded in what had been the Jewish section of town, the university eventually built other structures, including several student hostels and the law college mentioned by Schedel. Among the former were an endowed one for poor students; one for aspiring lawyers founded by the historian Długosz, who was also a canon in the cathedral; a building for wealthy students, in which they could keep servants and, if they needed them, special tutors; and a living unit for foreign students, especially Hungarians. The largest hostel was the one founded and handsomely endowed in the university quarter by Bishop Zbigniew Oleśnicki of Kraków, Poland's first cardinal.

Unlike the fourteenth century university, the fifteenth century school prospered. It was given endowed livings to be held by faculty, and several chairs were established for professors in such disciplines as rhetoric and astronomy. Students also came to the school in considerable numbers. Although enrollment dropped as low as thirty-five new matriculations in the fall of 1408, by the last decade of the century an average of 296 enrolled annually. In the first one hundred years of the school's functioning, more than 18,600 students attended one or more years. They came from throughout the kingdom and from many foreign countries. A significant number of them continued beyond the bachelor's degree to take one or more higher degrees.

The professors at the university were active in the national life of the country. They served the king, as when rector Paweł Włodkowic (Paul Vladimiri) argued before the Council of Constance that Poland's arch-enemy, the Knights of the Teutonic Order, should be condemned by Christendom and their order dissolved. They served the city of Kraków, as when professors such as Jan z Reguł (John of Regulus), a member of the medical faculty, was elected to the city council. They served the church, as when professor of theology and former rector Tomasz Strzempiński became Bishop of Kraków; or they served the ideals of the church, for which professor Jan Kanty was eventually canonized. And they served the national unity of Poland, as when Jakub Parkosz prepared a work trying to standardize the Polish language and its orthography, or when professor, many-time rector, and sometime Vice-chancellor Jan z Dąbrówki (John of Dąbrówka) prepared a textbook in the form of a commentary on Polish history which emphasized patriotism and moral virtue. But the greatest accomplishments of the university came in its function as an intellectual center. Its theologians refined and defended conciliar theory within the church; its natural scientists undermined the Aristotelian approach to the external world; its mathematicians and astronomers made the school an international center of learning in this field by the end of the fifteenth century; and its professors in all faculties introduced and supported humanistic interests in Poland, thus drawing to the city such noted figures as the German poet and humanist Conrad Celtis and the English humanist Leonard Coxe. The latter praised the school in a panegyric in 1518, asking that he be counted among "the sons of such an illustrious mother."

Kraków achieved its great flourishing under the Jagiellonians. With the extinction of that dynasty, the city entered into a period of decline. This may be traced to several factors. Changes in the European economy, particularly the trade routes, reduced Kraków's importance as a commercial center. The Polish gentry pursued a political program within the national government which discriminated against urban development and commercial activity in order that they might enhance their own position in the state; their success was Kraków's eventual ruin. The university, which had achieved such greatness between 1400 and 1550, became increasingly rigid and backward in its teaching, and soon degenerated into a social finishing school for sons of the nobility rather than being an institution of learning. Finally, for political reasons, the kings of the seventeenth century concentrated upon the Baltic to a very great extent, and after 1609 they moved the royal capital to a city which hitherto had had only regional importance, Warszawa (Warsaw). Gradually, Kraków became a provincial backwash. The next centuries were not happy years in the life of the city.

KRAKÓW IN MODERN TIMES

Despite this decline, Kraków has by no means been untouched by the dramatic events and personalities which have dominated the modern era. In every century it has known a moment or more when it played a role that took it to the center of the stage of history. During the seventeenth century, there flowed over Kraków part of the deluge of foreign invasions described so convincingly in the novels of Henryk Sienkiewicz. Swedish soldiers penetrated deeply into the country in a campaign that brought them to Kraków. There they wreaked enormous havoc upon the city. Buildings and treasures were destroyed, and priceless books and manuscripts in the university were burned and looted. Only the heroism of the citizenry prevented more damage to the city.

In the eighteenth century, the aftermath of the partitions of Poland again brought drama to Kraków. One of the heroes of the American revolution, Tadeusz Kościuszko, who had returned to his native land, was moved to action by his conviction that a free nation was invincible even when opposed by the great powers. On the morrow of the partition of 1792 he helped plan an uprising against the Russians. On 24 March 1793 Kościuszko proclaimed an act of insurrection in the market square of Kraków and as self-styled "Commander-in-Chief of the National Forces" took a dramatic oath of eternal loyalty to his nation. He declared that the "right of resistance against tyranny and armed violence" was the right of the Polish people. His cause ultimately failed, and although he never said the words *Finis Poloniae* which have been attributed to him, it was indeed the ''end of Poland'' for a century and a third.

Kraków, however, experienced some brief revivals in these years. Part of Napoleon's Dutchy of Warsaw (Księstwo Warszawskie) between 1807 and 1815, it became a Free City in the aftermath of the Congress of Vienna. This autonomous status was gradually destroyed by the occupying powers, especially Austria, and in November 1846 the city was incorporated into the Habsburg lands. This came, however, only after another dramatic outbreak of revolutionary activity. For a brief ten-day period in February, the Republic of Kraków (proclaimed under the guidance of the radical agitator E. Dembowski) fired the imagination of Europe. The exhilirating ''springtime of the peoples,'' as the era of 1846 to 1848 came to be known, soon gave way to the grey depression of subjection to Austria. Kraków was not even the most important city of Austrian Galicia. That role was held by Lwów (Lemberg). But the power of Polish sentiment and the heritage of the past was still present in Kraków, as was shown in 1869.

In that year, Kazimierz III Wielki was briefly resurrected. Workmen doing restoration work in Saint Wacław's cathedral inadvertantly broke through a wall in the tomb of the monarch. Inside were Kazimierz's remains, together with royal insignia and paraphernalia. Various officials of the cathedral chapter and the Kraków Society of Learning were immediately contacted. They eventually decided to have the great artist Jan Matejko sketch the interior, then to remove the remains until the tomb was renovated, and eventually to rebury them in a special ceremony. (The famous painting of Kazimierz which Matejko included in his series on Polish monarchs thus has considerable reliability, for the crown, scepter, and other insignia depicted in it are faithful reproductions of what the artist observed inside the tomb. In addition, his depiction of a long, flowing beard and hair is based upon the fact that remnants of these were still attached to Kazimierz's skull.) Ordinarily an event such as this would have been only of antiquarian interest. But the nineteenth century in Poland and Kraków was not an ordinary time. The memory of national freedom was kept alive in schools, churches, and scientific societies and by the agitation of a series of patriots. Not long before the opening of Kazimierz's tomb, Poland had again been convulsed by revolutionary uprisings, the disastrous revolts and insurrections of the early 1860's. These had eventually been repressed with considerable severity.

The decision to make the reburial of Kazimierz a special occasion evoked a great outpouring of national sentiment, not only in Austrian Galicia but throughout partitioned Poland. There was much discussion of the significance of the king's reign, with newspapers both carrying the reports of this debate as well as fueling it by fiery polemics of their own. The Jews of Kraków commemorated Kazimierz's time with solemn ceremonies in the synagogue. In the face of this enthusiasm, authorities representing the partitioning powers expressed some uneasiness. Eventually Polish representatives from all parts of the country, except Russian Poland, were allowed to attend the ceremonies and participate. Early on the morning of 8 July the dignitaries assembled. A solemn mass was celebrated at Saint Mary's church, with all who could not squeeze inside standing in a throng on the central town square. This was followed by a procession, with the body of the king born aloft in a new casket. This wound its way through the city and eventually arrived at Wawel. In the cathedral, where admission was only for those who possessed a card issued by the president of Kraków, another religious service was held. The comments made by participants in this were heavily tinged with the perspective of historical reference. Then the royal remains were reconsecrated and reburied. Tens of thousands who could not participate inside stood outside. The greatness of Poland's past, personified in this instance by Kazimierz the Great, was a source of strength for those who knew only the reality of the present. This event was a mass demonstration of the power of historical memory to enliven, inform, and inspire the present. It was understandable that the great powers were apprehensive about the potential inherent in such an historical celebration.

Another event during the nineteenth century was far less dramatic, but it also contributed to marking a stage in the city's history. In the early part of the century the town walls were pulled down. In the eyes of the Austrians, Kraków no longer needed to defend itself. Of the earlier fortifications, only the Barbican and a fragment flanking Saint Florian's gate remain. This passing of the past eventually brought with it an addition which contributes greatly to the charm of the contemporary city. Where the walls had been, a circular band of green park was built. Today it defines, just as surely as the earlier bastions, the old city. In this park (the *Planty*), one may wander slowly through the memories which haunt this "most illustrious city," pausing for a hot glass of tea in the shadow of a monument commemorating Jadwiga and Jagiełło or sitting on a bench to read one of the lively political or literary magazines which reflect the continuing vitality of the community there. One's reverie might be broken only by persistent pigeons seeking food or by the limpid sound of the hourly *hejnał*, conjuring up the memory of barbarian Mongol attack.

Not all the memories connected with the city are pleasant. In the twentieth century, new barbarians came to Kraków. Nazi hordes, brought by the horrors of modern military technology, set up their headquarters in the former Polish capital. From there they intended to direct the reduction of Warszawa to a village (they at least succeeded in reducing it largely to a rubble), the subjection of Poland to German control, and the transformation of Kraków, upon orders from Hitler, so that it would "become a German city." The royal castle on Wawel became the seat of residence for Governor General Frank, and such treasures as the

Stwosz altar were dismantled and prepared for shipment to Nuremberg and other German cities. The population of the city was drastically reduced by voluntary out-migration to the countryside, by losses suffered in battle, and by the system of deportation, forced labor, and extermination which the Nazis employed. Nearly all the Jews of the city were eventually executed, most of them at the death camp in nearby Oświęcim (Auschwitz). In the nightmare years of the war, Kraków survived. Those of its people who could, and there were many, worked heroically in the underground opposition. They utilized the methods of subversion against, non-compliance with, and the preservation of internal integrity in the face of, a totalitarian regime which they had learned to apply in those earlier decades when Poland had been merely an historical expression, albeit one of explosive potential. When the end of the war came, it came so quickly to Kraków that none of the city was destroyed, either in a scorched-earth policy or by the carnage and trauma of battle. Kraków remains today the medieval and Renaissance city of the Piasts and Jagiellonians.

Not all that is Kraków, however, is from the past. There are modern buildings (even a Holiday Inn!), new churches have been built in this century to complement those of earlier generations, and the growth of the city in concentric circles around its historic core the old town, a process which began in the nineteenth century, has continued apace. All of this would be expected in modern, industrial society. But some of the changes to the city are the direct result of the altered political, social, and economic conditions of the most recent decades. One of the more striking elements of this has been the creation of a second urban "core" for Kraków. Some kilometers to the east of the central town square, the government of Poland has built a huge steel foundry and furthered the growth of a planned community in conjunction with it, called Nowa Huta. This area now numbers more than ten times the population of medieval Kraków. It was the hope of the regime that this would transform Kraków into a worker's city. This has not yet happened, perhaps because the traditions of old Kraków are too strong, perhaps because Nowa Huta was established slightly too far away from the original settlement and is too self-contained. But it is still a part of Kraków, and one of the ways in which the traditions are continued is reflected by the following. One of the most recent buildings in Nowa Huta is a parish church, small in comparison with the sterile rows of faceless, impersonal apartment blocks which seem to tower over it. But in size, it dwarfs any of the older parish buildings in Kraków, and it holds the thousands who come to worship there. It is more nearly the size of a medieval cathedral. Fittingly, it was a successor of Bishop Stanisław in the See of Kraków who came to consecrate it when it was dedicated recently.

PAUL W. KNOLL

Los Angeles, California

Introduction:
The Nuremberg Chronicle

THE EXCERPTS from the *Nuremberg Chronicle*, a historical compilation written in Latin almost five hundred years ago, have a special meaning for this book. Hartmann Schedel (1440–1514 A.D.), author of the bulky *opus*, a thick folio of 326 leaves, is summoned as an impartial and neutral witness to present testimony on the life, death, and cult of Saint Stanisław in the medieval city of Kraków.

Schedel was not a naïve and poorly educated chronicler, compiling bits and pieces of interesting stories which attracted his attention, like hundreds of like chroniclers during the Middle Ages. He was extremely well educated. After receiving a basic education in his native Germany, he went to Italy to study medicine in the famed school in Padua. In addition to his successful mastery of medicine, he was also versed in astronomy, astrology, law, and theology. When he set himself to work on his *Chronicle*, he travelled widely, conducted research in many monasteries, attended courses in various universities, and transcribed hundreds of manuscripts. He was, indeed, a scholar.

A city physician with a large practice in Nuremberg, deeply religious, a devoted family man, in the later years of his life he conceived of the idea of writing a history of the world from the Creation to his own time. It was a bold and extraordinary undertaking.

Although Schedel never visited Poland, in Latin *Polonia*, but referred to in his work as *Sarmatia*, that country at the time was ruled by the mighty Jagiellonian dynasty. It was a powerful commonwealth, equal in prestige and influence to contemporary France, Germany, and England, as one can easily detect by observing the number of pages in the *Chronicle* devoted to the histories of these countries.

Schedel's presentation of Kraków, the capital of Poland at the time, with the oldest illustration of the city in existence, which appears in the *Chronicle*, is not only historically valid but often touching. He describes not only the city's monumental churches, monasteries, "the enormous royal castle, the beautiful and notable houses" of the citizenry, but the wonderful people that dwelled therein. With obvious affection and appreciation he wrote: "Kraków has the most illustrious citizens, notable for virtue, prudence and courtesy, offering gentleness and hospitality to every traveler freely and intimately."

But Schedel's greatest praises were given to the Jagiellonian University, one of the oldest in Europe, founded by King Kazimierz III Wielki in 1364. It was "filled with many famous, learned men who taught the liberal arts, rhetoric, poetics, philosophy, and physics." Special praise was given by Schedel to astronomy. He recorded: "Astronomy is here the most highly developed science. In the whole of Germany (and I know this from more than one source) one cannot find a more famous school."

When Schedel wrote those lines on astronomy, a keen student from Toruń was sitting on the bench of the *Collegium Maius* who showed particular interest in what was then known about the planets, the sun, and the stars. His name was Mikołaj Kopernik, Nicholas Copernicus. His great book, *De revolutionibus orbium coelestium*, a book that "moved the earth and stopped the sun," was conceived in Kraków and published fifty years after Schedel's *Chronicle*.

In respect to Saint Stanisław, the presentation of his life, death, and cult does not have another parallel in Schedel's book. No other saint in his *Chronicle* is described with such deep faith, strong conviction of innocence and saintliness as the Bishop of Kraków; at the same time no other king, emperor or ruler is depicted as so vicious, despotic, and monstrous as the Polish monarch of Kraków.

In this particular treatment, Schedel is no mere chronicler registering objectively a historical event, but rather a highly emotional writer; better yet a playwright. Thanks to his vivid and imaginative description, we seem to be with him 900 years ago in Kraków. There we witness the horrible crime committed by the ruler. We seem to hear the warnings of the saintly Bishop, uttered to the autocratic king, to amend his immoral way of life and to cease violating the human rights of "famous men and outstanding citizens." We can almost see the defiance of the king who not only "persevered in abominable and ugly debauchery but practised such treachery and tyranny upon his subjects," but who "committed even more atrocious deeds." Finally, like in an ancient Greek tragedy, came the climax: the bishop anathemized the king and the enraged king murdered him in the chapel of Saint Michał while offering the Holy Sacrifice of the Mass.

However, Schedel does not tell us that the king immediately fled the country and that he died doing penance in a monastery in Hungary. But he does confirm the cult, which was born instantly: "Stanisław was declared a saint, and his body taken in a golden sarcophagus into the royal castle to the church of St. Wacław, where he is famed for many miracles. The faithful venerate him everyday with frankinsense and prayers." Stanisław was declared the patron saint of the commonwealth of Poland. From there the cult spread to Lithuania, Byelorussia, and the Ukraine.

His successor in the seat of the Bishopric of Kraków, Karol Cardinal Wojtyła, commenced preparations in 1972 to honor the 900th anniversary of the death of Saint Stanisław to be celebrated on 8 May 1979, in Kraków. God in His Providence called Cardinal Wojtyła, on 16 October 1978, to rule the Universal Church from the throne of Saint Peter in Rome.

His Holiness decided to undertake a pilgrimage to the grave of the martyr in Kraków to commemorate the unique occasion of the anniversary of his death. In this commemoration the Holy Father is united with the whole civilized world which pays homage to his predecessor, who gave his life defending justice, morals, and human rights violated by an evil government.

The presence of the Roman Pontiff, Successor of Peter, His Holiness John Paul II in Poland, gives reassurance to his beloved native land and to oppressed people everywhere that the martyrdom of Saint Stanisław was not in vain: that despotism, immorality, and the violation of human rights by governments, throughout history, are always defeated in the end, and that the Divine Order, represented by John Paul II in Kraków, is ultimately victorious. The Cross which Emperor Constantine saw before the battle of the Milvian bridge, lo these many centuries ago, shines today brighter than ever with it's message: *In hoc signo vinces!* In this sign you will conquer.

BOGDAN DERESIEWICZ

Santa Barbara, California

S T. STANISŁAW, a man of great authority before God, is patron of all Sarmatia and her standard-bearer. He was born in the year of our Salvation 1008, in the village of Szczepanów, of parents belonging to famous gentry, whose concern was to attend divine services in the churches and to appease God by fervent prayers.

As a youth, Stanisław was sent on the advice of his father, to the famous gymnasium in Paris. There he studied the best literature very diligently, as the result of which he flourished with the greatest virtues, but he especially pursued sacred and divine law. Unlike contemporary lawyers who used to do it for profit, in order to reach a position of greater authority, Stanisław studied law so that, when the place, position or his rank should demand it, he could administer justice to the poor as well as the mighty and the orphans and particularly so that he could render to everyone fairly what was his according to the intent of the law.

Finally returning to the paternal abode, he came to Kraków, the famous city of Sarmatia. Here he discharged the duty of canon, thanks to his virtue and deep knowledge. After the death of the bishop, he was declared, thanks to God's providence, bishop of the vacant seat. Stanisław, always maintaining his position in the best order, gave his attention to the development of holy religion and divine worship.

It happened one time that he bought a village from a knight; when the latter died, his friends tried to take back this village according to the hereditary law. Stanisław was not able to bring forth proof of the agreement and purchase because those people who knew enough about it were hiding, afraid of the insolence of the accusers. But the saintly man gave himself to prayers and fastings, confident in the power of God. When he felt that he was strong enough, he approached the grave of the dead knight from whom he had bought the village and after removing the tombstone and the sand, he called God as a witness and brought back to life the man who had been dead for four years. He brought him before the despot Bolesław because before him such cases were to be judged.

In the presence of the gathering of his adversaries and the aristocrats of the royal government he proved clearly how he had bought the village.

The cruel Bolesław persevered in abominable and ugly debauchery and practiced such treachery and tyranny upon his subjects. Famous men and outstanding citizens he tormented with execrable and horrible punishments. At last Stanisław, as Christ's prophet, came to the conclusion that he could no longer tolerate this state of affairs. Intrepidly he approached the king to reprove him in order that he might desist from this kind of behavior.

But the king committed even more atrocious deeds every day. Finally, he was excommunicated by the bishop. In a rage, not knowing what he was doing, he sent his attendants to slaughter the bishop in whatever place he might be.

At that time the saintly Stanisław had come down to the small chapel of Saint Michał, built upon a small rock in the city of Kazimierz, to offer there the Holy Sacrifice to God.

When the king's servants arrived, they tried three times to enter the small chapel but thrice fell upon their backs, struck down by the power of God.

As this news was brought back to the king, Bolesław hastened with loud screams to the small chapel, where he slaughtered the saintly bishop during the offering of the Holy Sacrifice with savage blows and fearful strokes. Afterwards the body was cut up into pieces by servants and thrown outside the city so that the birds might tear it up the more with their hooked beaks.

But by Divine Providence, eagles arrived to unite the precious body and protect it with the greatest diligence until the faithful themselves buried it honorably in the Small Rock chapel with the most solemn ceremonies.

Finally, Stanisław was declared a saint, as was mentioned, and his body taken in a golden sarcophagus into the royal castle to the Church of Saint Wenceslaus, where he is famed for many miracles. The faithful venerate him every day with frankincense and prayers.

First depiction of the city of Kraków, from *The Nuremberg Chronicle*

KRAKÓW, the famous city of Sarmatia (which is called Poland), is located on the bank of the Wisła River, not far from its source. It was founded by Krak, the first Duke of Sarmatia, and many writers have been of the opinion that he gave it his own famous name.

I thought that it would be wise to insert the story of the Royal City of Kraków into this notable work. According to Ptolemy, that excellent and lucid cosmographer, it was a famous city of Germany under the name of Corrodunum, but Strabo defines Germany as the land enclosed by the rivers Rhine and Elbe. For this excellent reason we regard Kraków as a Sarmatian City.

It seems important enough to have its history recalled from its origin; therefore, I decided to describe briefly first its location in order that no one should claim that I narrate fables in a rather ambiguous and facile manner.

It is surrounded with high ramparts, bulwarks and high towers, then by a low city wall almost ruined from age, finally by hollows and ditches which prevent easy access to an invading enemy. Some ditches are full of water filled with fish, while others are green with shrubbery and grass. Immediately beyond the rampart in the valley a small stream called Ruda flows around the entire city. It moves the mill wheels which grind and soften the wheat with rocks. Finally the stream provides the whole city sufficiently with water brought in through underground canals and pipes.

The city has seven gates. The citizens live in many beautiful and notable houses; we see also many large churches, especially the church of the Virgin Mary with the two very tall towers, located in the middle of the city. In the many monasteries live large assemblies of devoted, religious fathers. Attached to the church of the Most Glorious Holy Trinity is the order of Dominicans. In this venerable church the Blessed Jacek, a man of great sanctity, companion of Saint Dominic, diffuses the odor of sanctity. He performs many miracles, although not yet proclaimed a saint; while still alive he brought three dead people to life. At the church of Saint Francis have dwelt the order of Friars Minors of the non-reformed branch. We could list many more monasteries.

Not far from the gate of the Wisła River there is a church called Saint Anne's, where the Blessed Jan Kanty, a teacher in the famous gymnasium, is famed for many unusual miracles, although he also is not yet registered in the catalog of saints.

Close to this above-mentioned sacred church is the large and glorious gymnasium filled with many famous, learned men who teach the liberal arts, rhetoric, poetics, philosophy and physics. Astronomy is the most highly developed science. In the whole of Germany (and I know this from more than one source) one can not find a more famous school. Phoebus is venerated very much there, as he polishes and improves their immature minds. The illustrious Władysław, a famous King of Sarmatia, built this school with large sums of money and endowed it with privileges and large stipends, after he had defeated the coastal Prussian tribes in a savage war. Many famous memorials of this war are preserved to this day in the royal castle about which we will speak later.

The burghers of Kraków do not live according to Sarmatian customs, since the Sarmatians, if we are to believe the ancient writers, were a cruel and sluggish people. Kraków has the most illustrious citizens, notable for virtue, prudence and courtesy, offering gentleness and hospitality to every traveler freely and intimately.

Their food is much more sumptuous than in the rest of Sarmatia. Among every kind of delicate food, a drink made of water boiled with barley and hop is in the greatest demand. If taken according to need and what one is able to bear, there is nothing more appropriate for the nourishing of the human body.

Inside the city, beneath the royal castle there is another outstanding college, where the Academy of Law flourishes. On the north side of the city is adjoined a small town, called Kleparz, which is not even surrounded by the city walls. Nothing here is worth mentioning except the famous and venerable church of Saint Florian, who was a vigorous soldier of the Christian faith. King Władysław, whom we have mentioned, restored it with a canonry, other dignities and gifts, and then returned it to the care of the teachers governing the gymnasium of arts.

Rocks and bricks ascend there to such a height that they seemed to hold up the skies. Then, they were covered with sand and heaped-up dirt so that they created a huge hill, which on the north overhangs the city while on the other side, are the scenic snowy, high rising Carpathian Mountains.

The Wisła, a prominent European river and once the boundary of Germany, washes against the side of this hill. The river starting from a small spring in the Carpathian foothills swells more and more as it proceeds, so much so, that when it has grown with the heavy volume of waters coming down from the Pannonian Mountains, it carries down logs, gigantic trees and various wooden structures. Finally, when it has swollen even more from the rains and its tributary rivers, it floats down rafts and merchant ships to the Zatoka Gdańska in the German Sea. Here, finally, it loses its name, unfolding itself through three great foaming mouths.

On this hill a huge church was first built in honor of Saint Wenceslaus, the Duke of Bohemia. Here are to be seen the memorials and sepulchres, erected with great skill and curious art, and carved in marble and alabaster, of all the most famous men, who according to custom were honored with great ceremonies and public processions. In the middle of this church stands the memorial in which rests the gallant soldier of Christ, Saint Florian. On the same hill there are two venerable churches, of Saint Michał and Saint Jerzy. Here also are the notable palaces of the nobility and the residences of the clergy, who worship day and night in the churches.

Then, the enormous royal castle, composed of large miscellaneous buildings; here was the capital of the entire kingdom where the whole Royal Treasury was preserved. Here the princes were gifted with supreme power because the Royal Crown was kept here and watched by a large number of guards.

Away from the hill is the monastery of the Friars Minors who observe very religiously their rule. The convent of the Holy Virgins is not far from this monastery. On the opposite side, close to the bridge, is a famous hospital and the venerable church of Saint Jadwiga.

Kazimierz, located on the opposite bank of the Wisła was founded by the king of the same name; the river flows around the entire city after dividing below the royal residence, making Kazimierz almost an island. Here is the famous church of Saint Catherine the Virgin, where flourishes the order of Augustinians. Further away is the church called the church of Corpus Christi, where live the regular canons, and there are still many other holy churches.

There are still in existence the famous memorials from the ancient college built by the Queen Jadwiga, most unusual survivals.

Illustrious kings and princes in these cities accomplished many other famous deeds, but we decided, in the interest of brevity, to end the matter.

O ŚWIĘTYM STANISŁAWIE
Biskupie Krakowskim, Patronie Sarmacji

ŚWIĄTOBLIWY STANISŁAW, mąż wielkiej przed Bogiem powagi, jest patronem i chorążym całej Sarmacji.

Urodził się w Roku Zbawienia Naszego tysiącznego ósmego we wsi zwanej Szczepanowo, z rodziców wywodzących się ze sławnego, szlacheckiego rodu, których staraniem było oddawać się w kościołach służbie bożej i Boga zjednywać pobożnymi modłami.

Gdy Stanisław wyrósł na młodzieńca, wysłáno go z porady ojca, do sławnego gimnazjum w Paryżu, gdzie z wielką pilnością poświęcał się studiom literatury. Już w tym czasie zabłysnął wielkimi cnotami: szczególnie gorliwie przykładał się do studiowania kościelnych i bożych praw; nie dla zysku, jak to inni prawnicy tego czasu zwykli czynić, ażeby uzyskać wyższe urzędy, ale raczej, ażeby mógł w przyszłości, gdy mu wysokie stanowisko albo warnuki pozwolą działać, równo wymierzać sprawiedliwość, tak biednym, jak bogatym, sierotom albo zostającym pod opieką; i każdemu po równi wyrokiem przyznać, co mu się należy.

Gdy wreszcie Stanisław powrócił w rodzinne pielesze, udał się do Krakowa, sławnego miasta Sarmacji. Tutaj, dzięki zaletom swego charakteru i wiedzy otrzymał godność kanonika. Po śmierci biskupa zostaje powołany za zrządzeniem Bożej Opatrzności, na stolicę biskupią. Godność tę piastował bardzo gorliwie, starając się jak najwięcej rozszerzyć wiarę świetą i służbę bożą.

Gdy pewnego razu świątobliwy biskup kupił posiadłość wiejską od pewnego rycerza, który wkrótce potem umarł, przyjaciele nieboszczyka podjęli starania, żeby tę wieś biskupowi odebrać na podstawie prawa spadkowego. Biskup nie mógł się wykazać dokumentami umowy i kupna, gdyż ci, którzy byli w tej sprawie należycie zorientowani, ukrywali się z obawy gwałtu od oskarżycieli.

Ale mąż święty trwał w modlitwach i postach; ufny w najwyższą bożą potęgę, która już tak długo go strzegła, przystąpił do grobu zmarłego rycerza, od którego tę wieś kupił, odsunął kamień grobowy i piasek, wezwał Boga na świadka w gorącej modlitwie i nieboszczyka do życia wskrzesił, który już cztery lata przebywał w grobie. Stanisław przyprowadził wskrzeszonego rycerza przed oblicze despotycznego Bolesława, stosownie do obowiązującego prawa. Tutaj w obliczu swych przeciwników pozostałych możnowładców Królestwa, wyraźnie dowiódł, jak tę wieś kupił.

Jednak gwałtowny Bolesław trwał uporczywie w obrzydliwym i nieprzyzwoitym trybie życia; stosował w pełni nierzetelność i samowładztwo względem swoich podwładnych; strasznymi i zbrodniczymi karami dręczył mężów znakomitych i obywateli nieskazitelnych.

Stanisław więc, jako przystało na proroka Chrystusowego osądził, że już dłużej nie powinien tolerować tego stanu rzeczy. Udawszy się więc do króla, nieustraszony zganił go i zażądał od niego, żeby zaniechał takiego postępowania. Król jednak popełniał co dnia coraz więcej zbrodni. Biskup wreszcie rzucił na niego ekskomunikę. Na to despotyczny Bolesław wpadłszy w ślepą furię, posłał swe sługi z rozkazem, aby biskupa zamordowali tam, gdzie go znajdą. O tej właśnie porze świątobliwy Stanisław udał się do kaplicy św. Michała, zbudowanej ponad Skałką w mieście Kazimierzu, aby Bogu złożyc ofiarę Mszy Świętej.

Słudzy królewscy przybyli do świątyni i usiłowali trzy razy wtargnąć do jej wnętrza i trzy razy bożą potęgą odepchnięci, na grzbiet upadli. Gdy król się o tym dowiedział, wpadł z wielkim krzykiem do kaplicy, gdzie zamordował świętego biskupa, odprawującego Mszę św., zadawszy mu szereg okrutnych ciosów. Królewscy słudzy poćwiartowali następnie zwłoki i poza miasto wyrzucili, by dzikie ptactwo je rozdziobało. Jednak dzięki bożemu zrządzeniu zleciały się w to miejsce orły, które pozbierały cenne ciało w jedną całość i pilnie strzegły zwłok aż do czasu, gdy sami obywatele byli w stanie pogrzebać je z należną czcią i największym nabożeństwem na Skałce.

Stanisław został zaliczony w poczet świętych, jak już wyżej powiedzieliśmy, a ciało jego złożono na Zamku Królewskim w świątyni św. Wacława w złotej trumnie, przy której dokonały się liczne cuda. Wierni wyznawcy bez ustanku wsród kadzideł i modłów cześć mu należną oddają.

O KRAKOWIE
Mieście Królewskim Sarmacji

UWAŻAŁEM, że będzie nie od rzeczy, ażebym w tym poważnym dziele coś więcej powiedział o królewskim mieście Krakowie. Albowiem sławne to miasto należy do Germanii, według świadectwa Ptolomeusza, najlepszego i światłego kosmografa, który je nazywa Corrodunum. Strabo zaś ogranicza Germanię tylko do tego obszaru, który rozpościera się między Renem i Łabą. My więc sądzimy z tej bardzo słusznej przyczyny, że miasto to będzie miastem Sarmacji.

Myślę, że to miasto jest na tyle ważne, żeby jego historię powtórzyć od samego zarania. Postanowiłem pokrótce o jego położeniu coś niecoś powiedzieć, aby się nie wydawało, że fantazjuję, opowiadając zmyślone historie.

Kraków więc, przesławne miasto Sarmacji, (którą Polską zowią) jest położony nad brzegiem Wisły, niedaleko od jej źródeł. Krakus, pierwszy książę Sarmacji je zbudował i wiele źródeł podaje, że je swoim imieniem rozsławił.

Miasto otaczają zaraz od samego skraja wały, bastiony i wyniosłe wieże; potem niski mur, który był zrujnowany z powodu starości; wreszcie doły i rowy, żeby utrudnić dostęp wdzierającemu się nieprzyjacielowi. Niektóre były napełnione wodą obfitującą w ryby, inne zaś zieleniły się od bujnych krzewów i trawy. Poza szańcem, który się wznosi wsród doliny, płynie mała rzeczka, Ruda, opływająca całe miasto. Ta rzeczka wprawia w ruch młyńskie koła, które mielą i miękczą głazami zboże; dostarcza ona miastu wystarczającą ilość wody, sprowadzanej doń podziemnymi kanałami.

Siedem bram prowadzi do miasta. W mieście znajduje się bardzo dużo przepięknych i wystawnych domów mieszczan. Wznoszą się również ogromne, liczne świątynie, specjalnie świątynia Matki Boskiej, położona w środku miasta, z dwoma bardzo wysokimi wieżami. Widać tu również liczne klasztory, w których mieszka mnóstwo zakonników, głęboko Bogu oddanych. Przesławny zakon Dominikanów mieści się w świątyni Św. Trójcy. W tym klasztorze mieszka mąż wielkiej świętości, błogosławiony Jacek, który, chociaż jeszcze w poczet świętych nie zaliczony, zdziałał już liczne cuda; był towarzyszem św. Dominika i już za życia trzech nieboszczyków do życia przywrócił. Przy kościele św. Franciszka znajduje się zakon Franciszkanów niezreformowanych. I jeszcze inne liczne klasztory możnaby wyliczyć.

Niedaleko od bramy Wisły wznosi się kościół pod nazwą św. Anny, gdzie błogosławiony Kanty, uczący w sławnym gimnazjum tego miasta, wsławia się licznymi cudami, chociaż nie jest zaliczony w poczet świętych.

Obok tej świątyni widzimy potężne, sławne gimnazjum, które obfituje w bardzo sławnych uczonych; tutaj studiuje się bardzo liczne wolne sztuki, jak wymowę, poetykę, filozofię i fizykę, ale najwięcej kwitnie tutaj studium astronomii. Nie ma w całej Germanii (jak z relacji licznych osób jest mi to doskonale wiadome) od niej sławniejszej uczelni. Tam czci się bardzo gorąco Febusa, który nieokrzesane umysły młodzieży wygładza i czyni szlachetniejszymi. Świątobliwy Władysław, wielki król Sarmacji, wystawił te budynki za wielkie sumy pieniędzy, po odniesieniu zwycięstwa w strasznej wojnie, jaką prowadziła Sarmacja z nadmorskimi Prusami (z tejże wojny zachowało się aż do czasów obecnych na Zamku królewskim, o którym za chwilę mówić będziemy, bardzo dużo przesławnych pamiątek). Tenże sam król nadał tej uczelni wiele przywilei oraz obdarzył ją licznymi uposażeniami.

Mieszkańcy miasta nie żyją według obyczajów sarmackich; starożytni pisarze podawali, że Sarmaci to lud nieokrzesany i leniwy; tymczasem mieszkańcy Krakowa, to obywatele znakomici, wyróżniający się cnotami, roztropnością i grzecznością, okazujący ludzkość i ofiarowujący każdemu cudzoziemcowi, jak najserdeczniejszą i największą gościnność.

Pożywienie mają o wiele lepsze, aniżeli w reszcie kraju. Z wszystkiego wybrednego pożywienia Sarmaci przekładają nade wszystko napój; przyrządzają go z wody warzonej z jęczmieniem i chmielem. Jeśli ten trunek bierze sie stosownie do potrzeby oraz wytrzymałości danego osobnika, to niema innego napoju bardziej odpowiedniego dla odżywienia ludzkiego organizmu.

W środku miasta pod zamkiem znajduje się również inne znakomite kolegium, gdzie się pięknie rozwija akademia prawa i ustaw. Do północnej strony miasta przylega miasteczko, które nie jest otoczone żadnymi murami, a zowie się Kleparz (Clepardius). Nie ma w nim nic specjalnie godnego do opisania, z wyjątkiem wspaniałej świątyni św. Floriana, mężnego szermierza wiary chrześcijańskiej, którą świątobliwy Władysław, o którym poprzednio wspominałem, wyposażył w kanonie i nadał inne należne godności i przywileje; profesorów uczących w gimnazjum sztuk wyzwolonych wyznaczył do jej strzeżenia.

Skały i szkarpy wznoszą się tutaj na znaczną wysokość tak, że zdają się niebo podpierać. Usypano tu ogromne wzgórze przez nawiezienie piasku i ziemi, która od północnej strony zwrócona jest ku miastu, z drugiej zaś strony na śnieżne, wysoko się piętrzące Karpaty.

Tę stronę wzgóra opływa Wisła, bardzo znana i sławna rzeka Europy, która ongiś stanowiła granicę Germanii i Sarmacji. Ta rzeka wypływając z małego zbocza Karpat nabiera z biegiem coraz więcej wody tak, że już znacznie powiększona wodą spływającą z gór panońskich, niesie ona na swych falach belki, olbrzymie drzewa i rożnorakie tratwy. Kiedy wreszcie Wisła dzięki deszczom i innym rzekom jeszcze głębszą i większą rzeką się stanie, wtedy jest zdolna zanieść łodzie i handlowe statki wiosłowe do Germańskiego Oceanu, do Zatoki Gdańskiej, gdzie gubi swą nazwę, wpływając do morza trzema pieniącymi się odnogami.

Na tym więc wzgórzu znajduje się ogromna świątynia zbudowana dla uczczenia świątobliwego Wacława, księcia czeskiego, gdzie znajdują się grobowce i nagrobki wszystkich najznakomitszych mężów, dużym wysiłkiem i różnym kształtem wystawione, wyrzeźbione w marmurze i alabastrze; jest w zwyczaju, że oddaje się tym mężom cześć wśród wielkiego przepychu i zgodnie z rytuałem. W środku natomiast świątyni znajduje się sławny grobowiec, w którym spoczywa przesławny rycerz Chrystusowy, św. Florian. Są na tym wzgórzu również dwie świątynie, jedna błogosławionego Michała, a druga św. Jerzego. Znajdują sie również na wzgórzu wytworne dworce szlachty i mieszkania kapłanów, którzy odprawiają w świątyniach modły.

A wreszcie widzimy tutaj potężną królewską siedzibę, na którą składają się liczne, różne budowle; tutaj znajduje się stolica Królestwa, gdzie jest cały skarb królewski. Tutaj obwieszcza się książętom nadanie im najwyższej władzy, albowiem w tym miejscu przechowuje się pod największą strażą królewską koronę.

Poza wzgórzem znajduje się klasztor Ojców Franciszkanów Mniejszych, tworzących bogobojniejszy zakon. Niedaleko od tego klasztoru znajduje się konwent Świętych Dziewic. Naprzeciw niego przy samym moście jest znakomity szpital i świątynia św. Jadwigi.

Na drugim brzegu Wisły znajduje się sławne miasto Kazimierz zwane, założone przez króla tegoż imienia. Wisła po rozdzieleniu się pod zamkiem królewskim opływa go i niemal czyni go wyspą. Znajduje się tutaj piękna świątynia św. Katarzyny, gdzie zakon Augustynów się rozwija. Widzimy również tutaj kościół powszechnie nazywany kościołem Przenajświętszego Bożego Ciała, gdzie Kanonicy Regularni mieszkają. I dużo jeszcze innych gmachów możnaby wyliczyć.

Widzieć jeszcze można wspaniałe grobowce starego kolegium, już rzadkie, które zbudowała znakomita królowa Jadwiga.

Najznakomitsi królowie i książęta dokonali licznych i wspaniałych czynów w tych miastach od czasów najdawniejszych. Uznaliśmy jednak za godne położyć kres dalszemu opowiadaniu historii tego miasta.

EPILOGUE

COURAGEOUS sanctity is a rare quality in any human being of any age and country. This extraordinary attribute is beyond compare and is highly desirable for all human beings. Its value arises from the fact that it ennobles the human person who strives to attain it. Its desireability flows from the union it accomplishes between God and the human individual. Rightly understood and appreciated, it is an inspiration and a challenge to the human spirit. Saint Stanisław, Bishop of Kraków and martyr for the Catholic Faith, possessed courageous sanctity, lived it to an unusual degree, and died rather than compromise it.

The eloquent history of his life as well as the cultural and social atmosphere of the city which was his episcopal See are teachers for all men of goodwill. The lessons they teach are compelling. They can also be uncomfortable because they goad and test the human soul. We are grateful for the opportunity to learn. Now there remains the need to apply oneself to live out the positive lessons learned.

✠ THADDEUS SHUBSDA
AUXILIARY BISHOP OF LOS ANGELES